Anthony M Keiley

Prisoner of War

Five Months Among the Yankees - A Narrative

Anthony M Keiley

Prisoner of War
Five Months Among the Yankees - A Narrative

ISBN/EAN: 9783744759441

Printed in Europe, USA, Canada, Australia, Japan

Cover: Foto ©ninafisch / pixelio.de

More available books at **www.hansebooks.com**

PRISONER OF WAR,

OR

Five Months Among the Yankees.

Being a Narrative of the Crosses, Calamities, and
Consolations of a Petersburg Militiaman during
an enforced Summer Residence North.

BY A. RIFLEMAN, ESQ., GENT.

———•◆•———

PUBLISHED BY
WEST & JOHNSTON,
MAIN STREET, RICHMOND, VA.

PREFACE.

My publishers, in whose judgment I have a superstitious confidence, demand a Preface; so I must be pardoned for informing the reader—what I suspect he would discover as well without—that he will find in this Narrative a plain unembellished account of my experiences as a prisoner of war, wherein I have endeavored to confine myself to a simple detail of facts, avoiding moralizings, eschewing rhetoric, and modestly renouncing my privilege of criticising "the situation." I have written rapidly, in the midst of daily work which left me no time for even the effort to round my sentences, if I had the disposition. If any of my countrymen or countrywomen shall feel disappointment at the moderate quantity of horrors herein, let them remember that I profess only to give what I *saw* and *knew*, and not what I *heard*, however well authenticated; and as I write with a diary before me, which I kept throughout my captivity, I claim for my story the merit of literal accuracy, both of fact and figure.

Some will reproach me for not coloring my pages with hues drawn from the passions of the hour, and God knows there is material enough for a fiercer flame than any that rages in a Southern heart: others will challenge the propriety of certain praises of the conduct of some of my enemies. To the first, I answer that this story to deserve the confidence of the public, must be "an unvarnished tale," and to the latter I can make no better reply than the immortal sentiment of Pym, "I had rather suffer for speaking the truth, than that truth should suffer for want of my speaking."

So, wishing my readers the happiest of New Years, I felicitate myself that my Preface is happily over.

THE AUTHOR.

Petersburg, January 2nd, 1865.

CHAPTER I.

Absit Omen.—Twenty Thousand Cavalry Approaching.—A Grave Perplexity.—Ready for Action.

Young ladies who swear by Tom Moore and L. E. L., and are afflicted with constitutional proclivities towards dyspepsia and dactyls, are wont to affirm that the Fates provide monitory omens in every important or semi-important event of our lives, after the chivalric fashion of those blessed troubadour days, when from tournament to tented field, no contest was thought lawfully begun without the preliminary flourish of some stalwort Stentor, who, if I rightly remember my Froissart and Brantome, was uniformly chosen with an eye single to his strength of lung, and his proficiency in lying— the man whose herald shouted loudest and bragged highest, having achieved that *premier pas* which in virtue or villainy always *costs*.

There can be no more groundless fallacy. Dame Fortune commences hostilities in ninety per cent. of her wars without blowing a trumpet, launching a proclamation, or firing the mildest of blank cartridges across our bows, quietly ambushing the best of us in the most flowery vallies, buffetting and persecuting us to the top of her bent, without so much as "by your leave, sir."

Marvel not then, most considerate of readers, that the 9th day of June, in the last year of grace, dawned on me as on the rest of my fellow-creatures, in the vicinage of this ancient town of Petersburg, with as fair a face and as bright a promise as the best of her sisters in all that queenly Spring. No croaking crow cawed unusual prophecy of evil over our heads; no friendly geese cackled their "*qui v'la?*" to intruding barbarians, winning the immortal gratitude of modern Quirites: there were no portents in earth or air, and though on the day in question I came to exceeding grief, it must have been written for me aforetime—"*absit omen!*"

I was sitting in my office peacefully engaged in endeavoring to extract from the Richmond papers, just received, something like an idea of "the situation," when, as though our city were blessed with a patent fire telegraph, all the available bell metal in the corporation broke into chorus with so vigorous a peal and a clangor so resonant, as to suggest to the uninitiated a general conflagration. Not being connected with the fire-brigade, and being otherwise totally disinterested on the subject of inflammable real estate, I might have remained absorbed in my enquiries, and thus escaped my fate, (and you this pamphlet,) but for a general understanding, if not order, that this signal, theretofore consecrated to the annunciation of fire, should thenceforth in Petersburg, serve the purpose further of heralding the approach of another "devouring element,"—the Yankees. Thus it came to pass, that in most indecent haste I let fall my journals and hastened into the street, to learn from the first excited passer-by that the enemy's cavalry to the number of twenty thousand—so ran the tale—were approaching the city, and already within two miles of where my informant stood! The "usual discount" of seventy-five per cent. still left the tale uncomfortable to a degree.

"What forces have we on the Jerusalem plank road, (the road by which they were approaching,) do you know?"

"Not a————man except Archer's Battalion, and not all of those."

Here was what Bill Sayres would call "another bloody go."

Military criticism was however obviously out of place just then, though, like all my fellow Americans, I affirm my competence and claim my right to hold forth on that theme, so I turned the key in my office door,—destined alas! to remain untouched by hand of mine for many a moon—and calling by my home to replenish my commissariat, I sallied forth prepared (morally speaking) to do battle *a l'outrance*, against all comers of the Yankee persuasion, though they had been as numerous as Abe's jokes, or the leaves in that umbrageous Spanish valley which has done such incalculable service to simile mongers since the days of our greatest of great grandmothers.

Admonished by the example of Tristram Shandy, whose amiable desire to acquaint his friends and the world with everything possible to be known of himself, leads him into most indecourous developments in the first three chapters of his autobiography, I shall not undertake to explain, but only state the fact that I was at that time not in *"the service"* in any capacity—though it is due to my family and friends, to say that I was *not* in the Nitre and Mining Bureau, nor the editor of a newspaper. One result of this unattached condition was, that like "Black Dan" in the halcyon days after Tippecanoe was *translated*, I was somewhat puzzled to know 'whither I should go." Another difficulty was, the vagueness of my idea what to do when I got there; but as the place to be useful was obviously the line of the enemy's approach, I turned my face thither and soon found myself in the camp of Major Archer's battalion, where all was preparation. My first duty was to make intelligent choice between three specimens of smooth-bore military architecture, universally known in the army as "altered percussions"—guns originally with flint locks, and therefore demonstrably a quarter of a century old, but modernized by the substitution of the percussion hammer and tube. These hybrids, without bayonets, were the weapons with which that handful of militia were to resist (or fly before) the picked cavalry (and many regiments of them,) of the Yankee army.

One of these formidable arquebuses had a trigger with so weak a spring that the tenderest cap ever turned out of a laboratory would successfully resist its pressure: the second was so rusty, that its ram-rod shrank from sounding its oxydized depths, while the third, which had the "spic and span" appearance of an assistant surgeon or a regimental adjutant on his first appearance, proved on examination to be so bent and wrenched, that you could not see light through it when the breech-pin was unscrewed! I now began to be overwhelmed with apprehensions that I was destined to act exclusively as a lay-figure in the drama about to be put on the boards, and my vanity not a little recoiled from the prospect of playing dummy in the game, when a friend, commiserating my perplexity, handed me a gun left in his tent by a comrade who had gone to town "on leave" that morning, and who was not likely to return. I soon balanced the "provant" which filled one of my pockets with ammunition enough to fill the other, and accounting myself " armed and equipped as the law directs," I joined the nearest company of " local forces," and accompanied them to the earthwork, a few hundred yards in front of their camp, for duty.

CHAPTER II.

General Kautz Opens his Mouth to Gobble Petersburg.—A Modern Thermopylæ.—Pro Aris et Focis!—The Author —— Gobbled!

The sun was clambering up the sky—a figure which Astronomy has vainly tilted against since the Great Italian's day—and the town-clock had struck 10 many minutes before, when a pair of frantic videttes,—one of them without his hat —tore into camp on foaming steeds with the news that the enemy, not more than a half a mile away, were rapidly approaching in a body consisting of several regiments of Cavalry, and at least four pieces of artillery. Our "position" was an open earth-work—the front face of which was cut at right angles by the Jerusalem plankroad—a thoroughfare which some outside barbarians may not know, opens up to deserving Petersburgers the beatific vision of Sussex hams and Southampton brandy. This work intended to accommodate two pieces of artillery, but then all innocent of ordnance, was accompanied by a line of low breast-works running out on either flank to afford shelter to such infantry as might be destined to support the guns, while beyond, on each side, lay a level and accessible country inviting easy approach to man or beast. There was nothing in the character of the position to give the assailed any advantage other than that which the breast-work offered in case of a direct attack, the ground being almost a dead level in every direction, and when Major Archer, our commandant, disposed his little force of about 125 men along the extended line—600 yards, I presume—it was perfectly evident that 20,000 cavalry, or any respectable minority of the same, would make short work of us. In conformity to universal civilized precedent, the Major addressed us a word of cheer and counsel before he assigned us our position; but there was eloquence incomparably superior to all the witchery of words in the hundred homes which stood but a scant cannon-shot behind us, and in the reflection that, according as we did our devoir, to them and to hundreds more, there might be then and thenceforth grief or rejoicing. Small marvel then, that as I looked down our little band, sparsely stretched over our extended and exposed front, and noticed how well the best and noblest of our townsmen were represented in its ranks, I felt that they would give an account of themselves, that no wife or mother, sweetheart or sister, would blush to hear or remember, though every Cossack that ever swam the Don, should charge our line that day.

We had not long to wait: a cloud of dust in our front, told of the hurried advance of cavalry, and the next moment the glitter of spur and scabbard revealed to us a long line of horsemen, rapidly deploying under cover of a wood that ran parallel to our line, and about a half a mile in front of us. *Then we missed our cannon:* our venerable muskets were not worth a tinker's imprecation at longer range than a hundred yards, and we were compelled, per force, to watch the preparations for our capture or slaughter, much after the fashion that a rational turtle may be presumed to contemplate the preliminaries of a civic dinner in London A little of that military coquetry called reconnoissance, determined our enemy to feel us first with a small portion of his command, and on came, at a sweeping gallop, a gallant company of troopers with as confident an air as though all that was necessary was that they should "come" and "see" in order to "conquer." Every one saw that this was a party we could easily manage, and we possessed, therefore, our souls in great patience till we could see the chevrons on the arm of the non-commissioned officer who led them, and then there broke forth (from such muskets as could be induced to go off,) a discharge that scattered the cavaliers like chaff,—three riderless horses being all of the expedition that entered our lines. *This trifling event saved the city of Petersburg*,—what else it saved, let the reader ask himself!—for the Yankees now became convinced that no cavalry charge would frighten these ununiformed and half-armed militia-men from their posts, and that a regular infantry attack must be made. For this purpose, two regiments of their cavalry were dismounted and deployed on either side of the road, in a line double the length of our own, and it was evident that they had determined to flank us on both sides. The welcome rattle of artillery horses brought now a cheer to every lip as we observed two field pieces falling into position on our right, and the sharp shriek of a shell curvetting over the Yankee line, was an agreeable variation of the monotonous silence in which, to the right and left, their skirmish line was stretching away to encompass us. This occasioned another check, and provoked an artillery response, which continued for twenty minutes, with about the effect currently attributed to sacred melodies chanted in the hearing of a certain useful hybrid, deceased. But these were all golden moments for Petersburg,—cannon, and horses were pouring into town. Graham and Sturdivant's batteries were wheeling into position, and Dearing was hastening to the scene with his gallant cavalry.

And now came the serious attack: the enemy advanced, outnumbering us five to one and armed with the *sixteen shooting rifle*, thus increasing over fifty fold their actual superiority,—and there we fought them; fought them till we were so surrounded, that the two nearest men to me were shot *in the back* while facing the line of original approach; till both our guns were captured; till our camp, in rear of the works, was full of the foe; till the noblest blood of our city stained the clay of the breast-work as they gave out their lives, gun in hand and face foeward, on the spot where their officers placed them. Their faces now rise before me this summery morning in November, the calm grave countenances of Bannister and Staubley, the generous joyous frankness of Friend and Hardy, the manly conscientious fire of patriotism in all— Bellingham and Blanks, Jones, Johnson, and the rest,—all gallant gentlemen and true, one of whose lives was well worth all the Yankees from Indus to the pole: and I could but ask myself then as now, the prophetic question whose answer has in all ages sustained the martyrs of Freedom as of Faith —*can such blood fall in vain?*

One by one they fell around me—Bellingham the last— and as I turned and stooped to change his position to one of greater comfort, at his request, the enemy trooped over the earth-work behind me, the foremost presenting his loaded carbine, demanded my surrender with an unrepeatable violence of language that suggested bloodshed, and all avenue of escape being cut off, I yielded with what grace I could to my fate, captive to the bow and spear of a hatchet-faced member of the 1st District Cavalry, greatly enamored of this honorable opportunity of going to the rear.

He conveyed me to Major Wetherell, the Provost Marshal of General Kautz's command, who was gathering the animate and inanimate spoils of the day,—the latter consisting of our muskets, all of which, with utter disregard for their age and manifest infirmities, he incontinently smashed. At this point I had the satisfaction of seeing a Yank, whose haste to destroy our guns was so great, that he would not take time to withdraw the load, blow a hole in his thigh—an accident whereon his Yankship is probably moralizing to this hour.

One by one, other captives began to fall in and were arranged in line, and a more varied collection in the same compass, could not well be imagined. An inexcusable weakness, for looking at the ridiculous side of everything, overcame, for a moment, my apprehensions for the safety of the city, and my sorrow and shock over the loss of my friends, though the latter sentiment, has alas! received rude treatment many a time, and oft during this bloody war.

Several of my comrades were many years over fifty, while some had not passed their second decade, and their pursuits were as diverse as their ages. Although, so few in number, I noticed among my fellow-captives, tradesmen and farmers, clerks and school-masters, merchants and millers, manufacturers, and magistrates, a city chamberlain, a member of the legislature, and a chaplain! In the matter of uniform and soldierly appearance, we were as motley a crew, as the memorable squad of recruits that Sir John swore he would not lead through Coventry.

CHAPTER III.

General Kautz comes to grief—In the Chain Gang—First Sleep in vinculis—Kautz and the Author talk it over—No Result.

One of the regiments that had not been dismounted now gallopped up the road—all obstacles being removed and filing to the left set their horses' faces toward the city. The prisoners meanwhile had been all gathered together and an officer was making a memorandum of their names, when a shell came booming over us with a welcome whistle, for it betokened resistance at a point where we thought our city defenceless. Another and another! and emerging from the lane down which a few moments before they had turned with such evident anticipation of easy conquest, we saw the rear, now by a "'bout face," the front, of the Yankee column retreating with Gilpin speed! All thought of cataloguing us was now abandoned and with significant intimations of the need of haste, we were ordered under a heavy escort " back to camp." It was a little after twelve—for we had held our ground two hours—when we started on our devious way to the pontoon bridge that Butler had stretched across the river at Point of Rocks, and with but one rest before we reached the river we continued our toilsome march—the cavalry constantly urging us to greater speed. Once or twice I got a " lift " from some benevolent trooper, who recognized the difficulty which bipeds experience in matching the speed of animals of more liberal ambulatory endowments, and before we had gone very far the assistant provost martial, Lieutenant W. E. Bird, introduced himself by an inquiry after his uncle a well known citizen of Petersburg. This introduction was fruitful of certain liquid comforts to which it is needless to make more particular allusion, and long before we arrived at our journey's end we had established a *rapport*—a canteen being the *medium* —which I remember now all the more gratefully as death has proclaimed an endless truce between the Lieutenant and his prisoner. I have said we made one regular halt—this was within a half a mile of the river, and about 11 p. m., when we stopped to permit our captors to take a little refreshment. Here we were gathered together and counted, when to the surprise of some, there was one man missing. The roll was called and Rev. Mr. Hall, Chaplain of the Washington Artillery was found to be absent. He had come out to the trenches after the fight began, in order to bring news to a lady in Petersburg at whose house he was stopping, of the fate of her husband. Though unarmed, a non-combatant, and a mere spectator, he was seized by the Yanks, put into line with the rest and hurried off despite his protest. On the march I was introduced to him—misery acquainting us oftentimes with agreeble as well as *strange* bed-fellows, and found that he had serious apprehensions of falling into Butler's hands—a worthy whose tender mercies he had enjoyed in New Orleans, and whose character and acts he had charaterized in terms of just and indignant criticism in a publication in the Southern newspapers shortly after the Beast drove him from the city.

Unwilling, therefore, to fall again into that saint's hands, he contrived to escape by obtaining permission to ride in an ambulance which soon got separated from that portion of the column in which the rest of the prisoners were, and when the party stopped, he quietly slipped out of the wagon, plunged into the woods, the night being as dark as Erebus, and thus escaped.

The Provost Marshal's wrath was excessive and profane at this *contretemps*, and he endeavored to shield himself from the charge of neglect by insisting that Mr. Hall had given his parole not to attempt to escape—a very unlikely story—indeed simply absurd.

While stopping here, the rest of the discomfited Brigade overtook us, and filing by, crossed the pontoon-bridge before us. We followed them, crossed into Chesterfield county, tramping along a well beaten road lined with tents, and with all the appointments and appearance of a huge camp.

It was past midnight as we neared General Kautz's headquarters, some three miles from Bermuda Hundreds. A filthy log hut, which was used as a guard house, was pointed out to us, as our hotel, and foot-sore, and weary, and hungry and blanketless, we threw ourselves on the ground to take our first sleep as captives.

I had hardly disposed myself for a nap when I heard my name called at the door, and on answering, was invited to accept a blanket and a berth in the tent of my new friend Lieutenant Bird. I accepted *nem con*.

Of course I ought now to have spent at least an hour meditating on the stirring and unusual events of the day, planning measures of escape, congratulating myself on the safety of Petersburg, berating the Yankees or wafting to the sympathizing stars affectionate messages to—none of your business whom. Alas! with much humiliation do I confess, my hand on my mouth and my face in the dust, not all nor any of these things did I. Doffing my shoes—no old soldier sleeps in his shoes—I speak from two and a half years of experience—I stretched myself on the floor, wrapped a blanket around me, and with a "good morning Bird," fell straightway into so profound a sleep, that if eyes soft or stern flashed on me in dreams that night, they left no trace on my waking memory then, nor leave they any now.

It was broad day when I shook myself out of my blanket at the instance of a friendly-voiced son of Vaterland, who administered a little spirituous consolation, besides furnishing me with a bucket of water and a towel, and in a few moments I was ready for a visit to my comrades, whose complaints of their several discomforts during the night argued a very indifferent appreciation of the lodging accomodations of their hotel.

The gnawing claims of vulgar hunger soon however proved to be gifted with the swallowing power of Aaron's rod, and we refused to be comforted because rations were not.

It was quite 9 a. m., when a barrel of "salt horse" and a couple of boxes of "hard tack" were deposited at the door of our pen, and flanking them, was a keg of most odorous sour krout and a small supply of potatoes. And here, gentlest reader, after a fashion which, for thy instruction, I propose to pursue, generally, in this narrative, let me jot down from my note-book the reflection I straightway made on the uncovering of the sour krout. I find written as follows: "June 10th, 1864; the man who invented sour krout had but three senses."

To explain, much more to enlarge upon, the above text, would demand an amount of space not to be thought of in the present condition of the rag market.

We were dividing out our "provender" with soldierly equity, when, very much to my amazement, an orderly hallooed at the door that General Kautz wished to see *me*, and hoping that there might be some good news for the citizen prisoners, several of whom were in our party—possibly their release,—I abandoned my rations, (a folly, I confess with mortification,) and in a few minutes found myself in the presence of the celebrated raider. Kautz is a man of about five feet ten inches in height, I should suppose, though I only saw him in a sitting position, has a swarthy complexion, a square massive head, wears his hair and beard cut close, speaks slowly and thoughtfully, and has the breeding of a gentleman. He desired me to take a seat, offered a cigar, and we were soon engaged in a conversation which was protracted for a couple of hours.

I did not hesitate to tell him how insignificant the force opposed to him in his attack of the previous day was, and asked him with as innocent an expression as I could assume, why he did not enter Petersburg after passing us?

"Only because I did not know how I could get out again. The failure of the expedition on the river roads which was relied on to support me made it necessary to be cautious, and while I might have dashed into town and burned some property, I might have lost my command."

In the course of the conversation I learned that he was a West Pointer and the school-mate of General Pickett, as well as several other Confederate officers about whom he inquired. He was by education an infantry man, and observed that he thought the government had spoiled a good infantry soldier by giving him a cavalry command. I discovered also that the General was somewhat piqued at his failure to receive credit with the Southern people for what he had done. He claimed to have planned and led the expedition that resulted in Morgan's capture on the Ohio the year before, and yet had hardly been mentioned in connection with it. But what surprised him most was that in the late raid which he had made around the South of Petersburg, his name had escaped notice except in one or two instances, where *it was mis-spelled*, while the credit or discredit of the expedition was divided between Colonel Spears who served under him and General Custar, who was not present.

The alleged superiority of Yankee cavalry seemed to inspire him with great confidence in the early subjugation of the "rebels," and he did not hesitate to express the opinion that the war would be closed by successful raids, and by the greater efficiency and better discipline of that branch of the Federal service, in actual combat. I thought of all this with very unchristian satisfaction some months later, when Hampton entered the Yankee store-room and cut out splendid cattle by the thousand under Kautz's very nose, and again later still, a week or two, when Hoke captured his last gun, and sent his last squadron flying in irremediable confusion, down the Darbytown road, to the very foot of Birney's infantry.

One thing I found General Kautz fully impressed with and very frank to acknowledge—the splendid fighting qualities of the Southern people. "I may safely say this," he remarked in the course of our conversation, "whatever be the issue of this war, we shall have a higher respect for your courage and military skill for ever hereafter." He appeared very much annoyed at certain acts of outrage committed by his men in Greensville and Surry, on his last raid, of which he heard the first, as he informed me, from my lips, and deplored the impossibility of preventing such acts, especially among cavalry, where it is so easy to leave and return to the column, and so difficult for officers to prevent misconduct.

On the whole I was quite favorably impressed with my captor, and regard my interview as among the most pleasant episodes of my sojourn *in partibus infidelium*.

The arrival of Colonel Spears put an end to our conference and I returned to my comrades to find the hard tack dwindling, the potatoes gone and nothing left of the "krout," but an odor so strong and so diabolical that I am firmly persuaded he who examines that log hut a century hence will find that:

"The scent of the sour krout will cling to it still."

I had little time to indulge regrets, however, for before many minutes we were ordered to fall in for General Butler's headquarters, and our baggage being as scant as that of the Hibernian, who refused to buy a trunk, because, if he put anything

3

in it he would have to go naked, we soon got into line and a half-hour's march brought us to the head-quarters of the Beast—a personage who on many accounts deserves a separate chapter.

CHAPTER IV.

MAJOR GENERAL BENJAMIN F. BUTLER.

"—— A sedate, a thinking villain, whose black blood 'runs temperately bad."—CONGREVE. Double dealer.

Off for Butler's Quarters—Benevolence of Providence—Pen and Ink Sketch of the Beast—Dialogue—The Lawyer's Hit—The Contraband Question—Jus postliminium.

On approaching Butler's quarters, which were quite handsomely located, out of reach of all intrusion, the first thing that attracted attention was the presence and prominence of *the negro.* So far we had only seen one or two of the negro soldiers on duty at the pontoon bridge, and the night being as dark as themselves, we could with difficulty distinguish them, but *there* Abysinia ruled the roost. It was "nigger" everywhere, and altho' the white soldiers were obviously annoyed at the companionship, the terror of Butler's rule crushed all resistance even of opinion, and the colored brethren knew, and presumed on, their secured position and importance.

We were ranged out in front of His Majesty's tent, and there kept standing hour after hour, in one of the hottest suns that I ever felt in any month or at any place. Most of the party were men, past middle age, and with hardly an exception they had had but one meal, and that a miserable one for twenty-four hours. When I add that they had had two hours of fighting and at least twenty-five miles of marching during the same interval, and that a sufficient shade was within a couple of hundred yards of us, it may be easily imagined that our first impressions of "the brute" were not *couleur de rose* by any means.

The afternoon was about half spent, when an order came for the first three men in line to report to him, and as I chanced to head the list, I heard my name handed in first by his orderly, and was soon summoned into the General's presence. There were two other persons in the tent, one a clerk or amanuensis who recorded in short-hand the somewhat protracted conversation which subsequently ensued; the other a complacent individual whose only and obviously agreeable occupation consisted in admiring his new uniform. My eyes were of course fixed principally on Butler, and the first and most pervasive thought that crossed my mind was one of profound gratitude to God who creates no mortal enemy to man, without clothing it with features that excite the instant and instinctive aversion of the entire human race. How deadly would the cobra and tarantula be, if Providence had not made them as loathsome as they are venomous? To Benjamin F. Butler's face scarce an element is wanting of absolute repulsiveness. Rapacity finds appropriate expression in his vulture nose—sensuality in his heavy pendant jaws—despotism in his lowering eye-brow, and to these facial charms is added an optical derangement which permits him to scrutinize you with his left eye—the one he seems to place most dependence on—while the right, revolving in a different plane, and concerned, you would imagine, about separate objects—wanders away in another field of vision. Add to this a cool, audacious complacency of speech and gesture which assures you that he is on the best of terms with his portly self, and I fancy you will have a description which, if not accurate enough for photography, will at least, convince you that Nature has hung out the sign of villain in every lineament of the Brute's physiognomy. He has a large and active brain—far the most acute of any that New England has contributed to this war—a voluble tongue, pleasant voice, and can be, they say, as gracious as "the mildest mannered man that ever cut a throat or scuttled a ship." But the ineradicable expression of his features must excite suspicion if not aversion, however impartial the gazer. It is popularly supposed that his defect of visual arrangement constitutes his unattractiveness—but this is a mistake. Mere physical infirmity is only a negative evil to any man unless it constitutes him a monster. An ugly or deformed man lacks the endorsement of Nature, which smooths the way for his more favored fellow, but in time he counts for whatever he is worth. John Wilkes, who was toothless, cross-eyed and otherwise ugly, was wont to say (and cotemporaries assure us it was no idle boast) "give me twenty minutes conversation and I will beat the handsomest man in a race for the favor of the finest woman in England," and History is full of celebrated and attractive men, who were cursed with some personal drawback. Alexander was wry-necked, Cæsar bald, Hannibal and Claudus Civilis one-eyed, Homer, Milton and Huber blind, Beethoven deaf, Byron club-footed, Pope and Scarron horribly crippled, Alcibiades a stammerer, who could not pronounce "r," Ovid abnormal in the nasal department, Mirabeau pock-marked and "boar-headed," Atilla and Pepin dwarfs with enormous heads, Demosthenes wry-shouldered and a stutterer, Esop a hunchback, and the list might be extended to a greater length than is generally imagined, yet among these were some of the most popular, and agreeable, and beloved of the race. In the coruscations of the great Tribune's magnetic intellect, women forget that Mirabeau was a *fright*, as under the witchery of La Valliere's voice, men thought not of her painful lameness. But if Butler were an Antinous with his present *expression* of face, he might reasonably aspire to the presidency of the ugliest of all the Ugly Clubs. Certainly he is just the man who would delight to torture women—only, I presume, preferring if he could have the choice, the plundering of men. Reverdy Johnson hoped to be the Cicero of this Verres, but the catalogue of his satrap's villainies was so black that even his callous master could not stomach the exposition, and the obnoxious truths were suppressed. The experiment was repeated by the Yankee Virginian, but the Brute laughed at the helpless indignation of his feebler foe, and pursued his speculations and peculations in sublime indifference to all criticism that did not cut off his supplies.

That he established and maintained order in New Orleans and Norfolk, is undeniable—but it was such order as reigned in Sicily in days of old, and in Warsaw, in later times—the order of sullen, abject, physical fear—a political *coma*, which is itself death.

But 1 beg unlimited pardon, oh, impatient reader, for all this sermonizing. So, I give my prosy Pegasus a rowelling, whereat the old cob frisks his tail, and puts himself out for a faster pace.

Quite a lengthy conversation ensued between myself and Butler, (Mem. I have reflected on the subject and do not think common self-respect will allow me to place his name first.) which proceeded on this wise,—the clerk busily recording it all.

"What is your name?"

"Mr. Blank."

"Your profession or pursuit?"

"I am a lawyer."

"You were captured yesterday, near Petersburg?"

"I was."

"How many men were in the trenches with you?"

"About one hundred and twenty or thirty."

"All militiamen?"

"All, with less than half a dozen exceptions."

"And you repulsed, I learn, for two hours General Kautz's Brigade of Cavalry?"

"You have been rightly informed."

*　　*　　*　　*　　*　　*　　*　　*

(Here ensued certain energetic expressions respecting the aforesaid cavalry, which bordered on the extremely profane.)

"Well Mr. Blank,"—and here he slid forward in his chair,

till his head rested on the back, and lighted a cigar,—" will you tell me how many soldiers were in Petersburg at the time of General Kautz's first appearance?"

Now the truth was, that to the best of my knowledge and belief, there was not, at that time, in town as much of a soldier as would entitle the government to declare martial law, and every one knows a half a conscript would serve that purpose. So I bethought me that mystery was my cue, and replied with affected solemnity:

"I decline answering."

"Oh, you need not decline. I know there was not a soldier there."

"Well, sir, there is no need to ask, if you know; but I am curious to know *how* you know that?"

"By this infallible induction: if there was a soldier in town, no lawyer would get into the trenches!"

I joined in the smile that followed,—and which Butler enjoyed hugely,—more in compliment to the truth than the wit of his inference, and replied:

"You speak of Northern lawyers, I presume. We have contributed our full share to this fight for freedom. If I may speak of myself, I entered the service on the 19th April 1861, and thousands of the profession volunteered as early."

"Yes, yes, I understand all that. I volunteered three days before you, but *I never got into the trenches*, and by the help of Heaven, I never shall. That is quite another matter, you perceive."

He here took up a note from his desk, held it within four inches of his left eye—what marvel that a man should have a *sinister* expression, whose vision is left-handed?—and continued:

"I would like to know the position of your government, and particularly of your people, on the subject of negro exchange. I have just received this note from Colonel Ould, in which the question is not met at all, and it is now a month since I applied for a categorical statement of the position of Mr. Davis's government on this topic."

"As I have no official character, I am of course not entitled to speak by authority, and as to the President's individual views, I know nothing."

"Of course, sir, I know you are not a commissioner, but I would be glad to hear your views. I think a white man is as good as a negro, and would be willing to give one of your negroes, if a soldier, for one of my white soldiers. But your government takes the position that the negro is better than a white man, and you will not give up one of my negroes to get back one of your best soldiers."

"My government, I presume, takes no such absurd position—she merely contends that the right of property in a slave, is no more affected by his running away to your army, than by his flying to your states,—least of all by your kidnapping. You are entitled to demand the exchange of your negro soldiers, not slaves, just as England would be entitled to claim her Sepoys, and France her Algerines, in the event of war between us and either of those powers. But, both your constitution and your positive statutory enactments, guard the title of the owner against disturbance from any quarter without the jurisdiction of the master's state."

"Ah, yes, but that is the law of peace. You claim the slave as a chattel: now, if I capture land and it is re-captured, it reverts to the original owner, but if I capture a chattel, a house for example, on its recapture it becomes the property, *not* of the original owner, but of *your government*, and is doubtless so treated. Thus the capture of *realty*, divests title only during occupancy; the capture of *personalty*, divests it forever. How do you make the slave an exception?"

"There is plainly no reason in the nature of things, why one description of property should be less sacred than another, and the discrimination against personal property only arises, I presume, from the difficulty of identification,—which does not exist in the case of the slave. Hence, the Roman law, if I rightly remember, excepted slaves, and common sense excepts them. So, I presume, would any property be treated that could be easily and certainly identified. For example, a Federal general goes to New Orleans, or Norfolk, and steals my house and all that it contains,—furniture, pictures, clothing, jewelry, everything,—but before he has a chance to send them to his wife in Boston, or New York, the city is re-captured, I presume my government would restore me my house with all its contents, and the conquering general would hardly think of holding an auction on my premises."

"I am not certain that he would not have the right. But how do you answer this? Public law authorizes the United States to declare that a slave fleeing to her shall be free: she so does declare in the case of every slave that comes to her."

"I answer that by denial, first of the fact and then of the right. And though both were true, I do not see how they could affect the power of our own government and laws, to re-establish the original relation, when all parties come again within their jurisdiction."

"Well, sir, it is to be regretted that our governments cannot agree about this, as there will be no more exchange, and no communication till the point is yielded."

"How is it then, General, that while you made this demand on my government a month ago, you continue to communicate, as I see from Colonel Ould's dispatch?"

"Oh, Mr. Davis moves very slowly, and I was giving him time to make up his mind. He has now had abundant time, and I am going to stop all intercourse."

Our conversation then took quite a wide range, during which I re-called to his memory his own secession at Baltimore, from a certain Democratic convention, and indulged in some references not altogether complimentary to the cruelty and avarice* of Federal generals. This seemed to provoke his wrath, and he dismissed me with the emphatic and disagreeable instruction, that my imprisonment would end with the war! *Diis aliter visum*, my dear Brute.

CHAPTER V.

To Bermuda Hundreds—The "Orderly" Disease—Under Negro Guard—A Cold Nap—Down the James—Falling among Thieves—Off for Point Lookout.

I was now dismissed, and two or three of my comrades successively summoned before him, but he contented himself, as they told me, with a question or two, respecting the number of our soldiers in the city.

The scorching sun was well on the wane when we again struck the trail,—this time for Bermuda Hundreds, some two miles off. Sundry mounted officials passed us, wondering very much at the civilian appearance of our squad, and I began then to observe the first indications of the "orderly" epidemic which I afterwards found to be a universal affliction of the Yankee military. Every one has an "orderly," from the Lieutenant General, down to the most subordinate pedler in tracts and ginger-bread, that wears the badge of the Sanitary or the Christian commission. To ride a mile without an obsequious varlet in your wake, whose chief

---

* The rapacity of the New England generals is conspicuous. Butler is omnivorous, but Neal Dow's passion was *furniture*. Being quite ill once, one of his officers asked the surgeon who attended him, what was the matter? "Only an unusual meal of furniture; but as I got him to throw up a bureau and a rocking-chair, I think he will recover," was the reply. It was a standing joke among Western soldiers, that General Dow had furniture (as Butler has nigger,) on the brain.

4

business seems to be to intercept the mud from your horse's heels, is a humiliation which no "free and equal" cavalier of the Great Republic could brook an instant; so, from commissary to commander-in-chief, there's a Sancho for every Don. I attributed this weakness to the novelty of the position of most of these Yanks. To the Southern people their education and labor-system gives the habit of command, and they attach little importance to the possession of a servant, from the generality of the fact of such possession. But most of the Yankee centurions never before had the power to say to this one, "go," and to that one, "come," and to the other, "do this," and as all essentially vulgar minds take delight in the parade of such a power, it is not, perhaps, surprising that these Cedrics make a show of their "born thralls" on all occasions; and, sooth to say, Gurth wears his collar with most servile satisfaction.

Past these masters and serfs, past crowds of sutlers and camp followers, past rows of grinning Ethiops, dirty, oleaginous, and idle, we wended our way to the river, which soon was marked out to us by scores on scores of masts, and as twilight fell upon us, we arrived in front of a Provost Marshal's office, where we answered dutifully to our names and were turned over to a new authority. A frame building, whose only other tenant was a negro in irons, was allotted to us for the night, and stationing myself in a window, I began, in the little light still left, to amuse myself with drawing a crayon likeness of Butler, when, for the first time, I noticed that our new guards were *black!* An odorous Congo, with a claymore two-thirds his length, a Nubian nose, boundless buttons, and the port of Soulouque was strutting up and down before me in most amusing enjoyment of his responsible position. Like every other negro soldier I met, with three exceptions, he was as black as Mason's "Challenge," and as surly looking a dog as ever brake bread. Before he had been on duty ten minutes he picked a quarrel with a brother black who dared to cross his post, and straightway both drew their sabres to my infinite satisfaction, as I presumed I was about to be favored with a sample of ebony chivalry according to "the code," but I soon found, to my great grief, that the sabres were only designed to give impetus and a finish to a fusillade of oaths, which, for number, force, and unrelieved profanity, I never heard equalled but once. On our return from Gettysburg, while crossing the mountains, I saw a first class army "stall,"—scores of wagons blocked up in a narrow mountain-way on a down grade of about two thousand feet to the mile,—everything with wheels running into everything else, and a herd of Pennsylvania beeves filling up the small and constantly varying intervals between the vehicles. Then broke forth from the trained lungs, and exhaustless vocabulary of a hundred lusty teamsters, such a torrent, cataract, avalanche, wirldwind, yea, very "Cyclone" of imprecations as passed competition of the most terrible swearing in Flanders. The common expletives, in which surcharged gall finds vent with ordinary mortals, found no room in that Lodore of cursing,— they were obviously thought unworthy the occasion,—and a new set "*horrendum, ingens, informe,*" blasted the ears and eyes, head and heart, legs and body, mane and tail of every individual mule and muleteer in all that involved mass, while the interest of myself and my fellow-soldiers received a spicy fillip, from the fact that we had to creep round the edge of this struggling mass, which left but a few inches between the outside rank and an inviting precipice, a half a thousand feet sheer! Then only did I hear superior swearing, before or since, although, my experience therein, especially since my capture has been very large,—whereof, more anon.

Getting an old stump of a broom, I swept up a small space in one corner of our jail, and, without blanket or overcoat, laid my head on my arm and was soon asleep. The nights of June are proverbially cool, and our clothing being saturated with perspiration from the heat, exposure and exercise of the day, I fell into a dream of hunting Frankenstein through the North-West passage, in the midst of which I woke, just in time to save myself from a plunge through a treacherous seal-hole into the Polar sea! I found myself chilled through and stiff with cold. There was no fire to be had, and the darkey at the door incontinently refused to permit me to walk out, so I was constrained to restore circulation by certain frantic gymnastics, in which I was, before long, joined by sundry comrades similarly uncomfortable.

Like everything sublunary (except Coleridge's sermons,) the night came, perforce, to an end, and we were allowed to go out, two at a time, to wash our faces,—a rather superfluous ceremony in the *absence* of soap and towels, and the most striking *necessity* for both. Salt-junk, coffee and as much "hard tack" as we wanted, were issued to us by our "colored brethern," and at 8½ a. m., a guard of twenty, from the same regiment,—the 1st U. S. Colored Cavalry,—formed around us with drawn swords,—a white officer at their head,—and, thus convoyed, we proceeded aboard a fine river boat, the "John A. Warren."

A few minutes after getting aboard, an officer came from shore with a dispatch from General Butler, commanding the return of three of our party (whom he designated by name,) to his head-quarters. This manœuvre, I believe, never received satisfactory explanation: the men were detained several days by Butler, and eventually sent to the same prison with the rest of us. Before another half hour passed, we heard the tinkle of the engineer's bell, the gang plank was drawn aboard, the paddles began to revolve, lines were cast off, and we felt indeed that we were turning our backs on home. It was the "bluest" moment of my imprisonment. There seemed such a cruel injustice in tearing a party of men, some of whose heads wore the gray honors of many a winter, from families and friends, and all that men hold dear, for the crime alone of standing before their own hearths and homes, and resisting assassins and burglars, bent upon the desecration of both, that I called in vain on philosophy for consolation, and as we glided along by the well-remembered and ancient plantations of our beautiful river, seen then the first time for three years, and to be seen again——alas, when! I recalled the days when those deserted and wasted mansions were the abode of a courtly, generous hospitality, worthy of the baronial days of "merrie. England," until I filled my mind and heart with such memories and such regrets as are wont to moisten sterner eyes than mine.

We sailed past two long pontoon rafts, in preparation for the move of General Grant across the river, soon to take place with such pomp and trumpeting, past the cloud of transports, that the supply of his vast army, so soon to change its base, demanded; past the Atlanta, so easily captured not long before in the Savannah, and a little before 5, came abreast of Newports News, and in sight of Old Point and the *resident* fleet of Hampton Roads. When I saw that harbor again, there were two thousand guns upon it, and such an Armada as the world never saw before. Landed, we were again marched before a Provost Marshal, and required to answer our names, and then, under our negro guard, marched to camp Hamilton, a little West of the large structure formerly known as the Chesapeake Female College, of Hampton.

This "camp" is a two-story wooden barrack, with a small yard, the whole surrounded with a fence, some fifteen feet high. Into this enclosure we were marched, our line straightened out, and the perennial roll-calling again gone through with, and then we were dismissed and told to find room to sleep in, as best we could.

I had hardly left the ranks, when a jolly son of Erin—a Federal soldier—stepped up to me, beckoned me aside, and informed me that the lower story of the building was occupied by Yankee prisoners, incarcerated for various villainies, and that into that apartment I must, under no circumstance, venture, as they garroted and robbed every Confederate soldier they could inveigle into their den. I asked, with some surprise, whether complaint was never made. "Oh, yes," he said, "*greenies* do complain, and the officers laugh in their faces." I needed no further warning, and steered clear of the "below stairs" in that mansion. Five minutes had not elapsed before one of our party emerged from that lower door, swearing like an irate moss-trooper. One of the Yankees had offered him some coffee, for which he was of course very grateful, and invited him in to drink it; but he had hardly entered the den before a blanket was thrown over his head, and he was pulled to the earth, his pockets rifled, and even the gold buttons wrenched from his shirt!

I thought it time to get up-stairs among some honest Confederates, and so mounted to the second story, where I had the good fortune to meet two old friends who had been incarcerated there some time, and who having learned the ropes, had made themselves comfortable. They very kindly gave me a bunk and a good supper, for both of which they have now, as they had then, my benediction, and having washed my face after a civilized fashion, I turned in to a sleep which the excitements of the past three days made very desirable, —and very profound. The next day was Sunday, our first in prison.

"I think that those people, the rituals of whose churches comprise prayers for the captives, never utter those petitions with sufficient unction. I'll mend my fervor in that behalf hereafter." Such is the memorandum in my diary, under date of June 12th. I commend it pious reader of mine, to your attention—make a note on't.

There is, in the Roman Catholic church, an order called the Redemptorists, whose members, besides taking the usual monastic obligations of Poverty, Chastity and Obedience, also bound themselves by a vow, to dedicate their lives to the redemption of captives, particularly those taken by the Moors; and so faithfully did they devote themselves to this pious vocation, that in the event of any of them failing to compass otherwise, the release of at least one captive, he considered himself bound to volunteer to take the place of some christian prisoner thus confined, and restore him, thereby, to his family. Cases of this wonderful self-denial were of constant occurrence, and strange to say, the barbarians kept faith with the good monks with surprising scrupulousness. We concluded, while in bonds, that something of that sort was desperately needed at the present day, only the Yankees would scarcely be as honest as the pirates.

About sun-down, we were marched back to Old Point, and with a hundred or more compatriots, huddled into the bow of the "Louisiana," a well-known boat of the old Bay Line to Baltimore. Here it was our fortune to succeed in the tenancy of our premises, to an invoice of horses brought down by the boat on her preceding trip, and anything being thought good enough for the *rebels*, the ceremonies usual on converting a stable into a human habitation, were dispensed with! In these savory quarters we were packed away; the frowning fortress with her diadem of cannon soon faded into distance, and by 11 o'clock, we made Point Lookout. Why this cape is so called; I am at a loss to imagine, as there is nothing in the prospect to make the most curious inhabitant "look out" in any direction. This matter of nomenclature has puzzled wiser heads than mine, and I am free to admit that Point Lookout is far from an exceptional case. A certain group of islands in the Pacific is denominated "Society," because there is no society there, I suppose, and another, denominated "Friendly," although the kindest office the inhabitants perform to strangers is to eat them. Geography has many a *lucus a non lucendo*. The tide being down, we were landed by means of a little tug that came puffing and fussing alongside, and hungry, sleepy and half frozen, we set our tired feet on the friendly shores of "Maryland, my Maryland."

CHAPTER VI.

Out in the Cold—Searching the "Reb"—The Pen Condemned to the "Lyons·Den"—A friend in need—Prison Demoralization.

It was our misfortune to fall straightway into the hands of a polished scamp. It was scarcely midnight when we landed on a long pier, which jutting out into the Potomac caught the full sweep of the sharp Nor' Wester, that screamed and rattled down the channel of the river. The guard though comfortably clad and furnished with heavy overcoats, suffered acutely, and altho' the officer which met us as we landed told them that we could not be received until morning, the soldiers did not imagine that their duty required them to stay themselves, or keep their prisoners on the exposed extremity of the long wharf, and they accordingly marched us to land. Huddling ourselves together we were endeavoring to coax a wink from Morpheus, when some ill wind blew the receiving officer, Lieutenant Phillips, again before us. He straightway opened a torrent of profane abuse upon us and upon our guard, ordered them to take us inimediatly back to the end of the pier, and waited to see his orders executed, breathing unmentionable execrations against the whole of us. Shivering and utterly miserable, we were marched back, and spent the night in vain efforts to find heat in exercise—sleep being out of the question. The guards themselves with blanket and overcoat complained bitterly of the fierce blast, while we had to endure it in light summer costumes, some even without a coat or roundabout. The hours dragged heavily on, and not until 7 o'clock in the morning, were we allowed to come off the river.

Another Provost Marshal's office soon hove in sight, before which we were ranged in a double rank and the inevitable roll-call again followed. All being right, Lieutenant Phillips, our worthy of the night before, appeared again, rejoicing in mutton-chop whiskers, and a grape vine cane, and in a gruff, peremptory voice, ordered the first four of us to step out to be searched. This was accomplished by himself and a couple of assistants, and consisted in turning the contents of our pockets on the ground, and then taking off all our clothing except what was absolutely next the skin, *and part of that also.* This was done to enable the examiners to search thoroughly our persons for money—a commodity which was pretty generally stolen at Point Lookout, either formally or informally—and in case of Lieutenant Phillips, this ceremony was usually varied by tearing the lining out of the hats and pantaloons of such unfortunates as fell particularly to his lot. Some of his aids were discharging their duty too gingerly for his notions of official obligation, and hailing them with "that's no way to search d—d rebels," he proceeded to illustrate by unusual violence of conduct, what he thought the proper way—sundry seams suffered in *consequence*. This *rifle* practice having been continued until all our valuables were taken from us, we were graciously permitted to dress ourselves, and the line being formed once more, we were marched off a quarter of a mile to "THE PEN."

The military prison, or rather prisons, at Point Lookout, consist of two enclosures, the one containing about thirty, the other about ten acres of flat sand, on the Northern shore of the Potomac at its mouth, but a few inches above high-tide, and utterly innocent of tree, shrub or any natural equivalent for the same. Each is surrounded by a fence about fifteen feet high, facing inwards, around the top of which on the outer face, and about twelve feet from the ground, runs a platform on which twenty or thirty sentinels are posted, keeping watch and ward, night and day, over the prisoners within. Besides these precautions, a strongly fortified palisade stretches across the tongue of land on which the prisons stand, from the bay on the North East, to the Potomac on the South West. Within this palisade, but of course outside of the "pens," are usually two regiments of infantry, and a couple of batteries of artillery, and without the fortification two or three companies of cavalry, while, riding at anchor in the bay, one gunboat at least may always be seen. One face of each of these "pens," the Eastern, fronts the bay, and gates lead from the enclosures to a narrow belt of land between the fence and the water, which is free to the prisoners during the day, piles being driven into the bay on either hand to prevent any dexterous "reb" from *flanking out*. A certain portion of the water is marked off by stakes driven into the bottom, for bathing purposes, and most of the prisoners gladly avail themselves of the privilege thus afforded; although, as the same locality precisely and exclusively, is devoted to the reception of all the filth of the camp, I admit a squeamishness which deprived me of sea bathing as long as I staid there.

Allons mes amis! we have been outside as long as the gentleman of the grape-vine and mutton-chop will permit—let us enter.

The first thing that strikes you as peculiarly prominent within the fence is a row of eight or ten wooden buildings, jutting out from the Western face of the Pen, a hundred feet long, perhaps, by eighteen in width, and one story high, with four tables running down the entire length of each. At the end next the fence, a partition divides off about twelve feet of the structure. These are the Mess Rooms and cook houses. Here all the public cooking and eating of the premises is conducted. A street, twenty feet in width, runs along the front of these houses, and at right angles to this street, run long rows of tents of all imaginable pattern, and of no pattern at all, to within twenty or thirty feet of the opposite face of the enclosure. Each of these rows of tents is designed to contain one thousand prisoners, and at the time of our advent, there were ten of these nearly filled, and another just begun. We were assigned to various "divisions," as the rows of tents are called, and dismissed. I was informed that Co. "B," 4th Division, was my "command," and reporting forthwith to the Sergeant of the same, he designated my place as No. 15, in a dirty Sibley tent, which the tenants, from some freak, strongly suggestive of danger, however, had christened and duly labelled, the "Lyon's Den." (I disclaim all responsibility for the orthography.)

I approached the structure with about as heavy a heart as any unregenerate Daniel might be supposed to possess on presentation to a location with so fearful a name, but the sight that met my eyes as I stooped to pass in, barred my further progress. It is not necessary to enter more particularly into details than to intimate that my prospective mess-mates were anxiously on the war-path after certain animals of the parasite order, whose name—*infandum*—has the same origin as that of *la belle passion!* Marius, amid the ruins of Carthage;

Belisarius, begging the obolus; Coriolanus, when his ma was plaguing him, or Miss Gunnybags, in the first instant of her discovering that Flora McF's. lace was a half inch deeper than her own—not the grief of any or all of these, (except possibly the last,) could equal the mute misery with which hungry, sleepy, dirty, tired, angry, robbed, and rebellious, I stalked (if five feet, eight and a half *can* stalk,) away, with a sigh and a groan, from the "Lyon's Den."

I had not gone far before I was hailed by name in a voice perfectly familiar, though I had not heard it before for some time, and turning in the direction whence it came, saw a well known face, my vis-a-vis aforetime in many a game of "prisoners base," or "chermany," in the blissful days of boyhood. I think he must have known intuitively both the character and the depth of my misery; for his first question was:— "Where are your quarters." I mentioned the dread name with a sickly attempt at a smile, which was a signal failure, when, my friend, a ten months resident of the prison, invited me around to his *shebang* (*Anglice* domicile) until I could better provide myself. Several of my companions were similarly favored, and those who were not, were provided generally with new tents and allowed to make up their own messes.

Sleep was what I wanted most, so borrowing a blanket from my good Samaritan, I availed myself of his invitation, and before many minutes was happily indifferent to all terrestrial affairs. Physiologists have amused themselves with recording the order in which the several senses go to sleep: my own opinion is that, under such circumstances, they make a lumping business of it, and fall by platoons; certainly such was my experience.

I now began prison-life in earnest, and none but those who have experienced it can approximate an idea of its wretchedness. This did not consist in loss of liberty, in absence from home, in subjection to others' control, in insufficient food, in scant clothing, in loss of friends, in want of occupation, in an exposed life, in the absence of all conveniences of living, in the mental or physical oppression of confinement—though,

God knows, all these are bad enough, and contribute in the aggregate greatly to the enhancement of the misery of a prisoner. I think, however, that the great overshadowing agony of imprisonment is isolation.

>——————— the dreary void,
> The leafless desert of the mind,
> The waste of feelings unemployed."

The world, friends, fellow-citizens, home, are things as remote as though in another sphere. Death brings its compensation aside from the consolations of religion, in the remembrance that it is irreversible, and we choke down and eradicate, if we cannot exalt and purify those emotions, whereof the lost were the objects, insensibly changing our social schedule to meet the new order of things. But the prisoner preserves affections and interests without being able to indulge them, and thus with straining eyes and quickening pulse, he dismisses continually the dove for the expected emblem, but it returns forever with flagging wing and drooping head, not having found whereon to rest its weary foot. Thus, there comes that despair which is the aggregate of many, or the supremacy of one disappointment—and from despair comes always degradation. Men become reckless, because hopeless—brutalized, because broken-spirited, until from disregard of the formalities of life, they become indifferent to its duties, and pass with rapid though almost insensible steps from indecorum to vice—until a man will pick your pocket in a prison, who would sooner cut his throat at home.

I perceive, that I shall have to write a didactic chapter, however, and the reader may as well prepare himself for his fate. Meanwhile, I will continue my record of *the facts* of my prison experience.

CHAPTER VII.

Prison Programme—Miss Dix on the Witness Stand—Copperas Water—Under Water—Yankee Thievery—Guards and Patrols.

The routine of prison-life at Point Lookout was as follows: Between dawn and sunrise a "reveille" horn summoned us into line by companies, ten of which constituted each division—of which I have before spoken—and here the roll was called. This performance is hurried over with as much haste as is ascribed to certain marital ceremonies in a poem that it would be obviously improper to make more particular allusion to—and those whose love of a nap predominates over fear of the Yankees usually tumble in for another snooze. About 8 o'clock the breakfasting begins. This operation consists in the forming of the companies again into line, and introducing them under lead of their Sergeants, into the mess-rooms, where a slice of bread and a piece of pork or beef—lean in the former and fat in the latter being contraband of war—are placed at intervals of about twenty inches apart. The meat is usually about four or five ounces in weight. These we seized upon, no one being allowed to touch a piece, however, until the whole company entered, and each man was in position opposite his ration (universally *and properly* pronounced *raytion*, among our enemies, as it is almost as generally called, with the "a" short among ourselves.) This over, a detail of four or five men from each company—made at morning roll-call—form themselves into squads for the cleansing of the camp—an operation which the Yankees everywhere attend to with more diligence than ourselves. The men then busy themselves with the numberless occupations, which the fertility of American genius suggests, of which I will have something to say hereafter, until dinner time, when they are again carried to the mess-houses, where another slice of bread, and rather over a half pint of a watery slop, by courtesy called "soup," greets the eyes of such ostrich-stomached animals, as can find comfort in that substitute for nourishment. About sundown the roll is again called, on a signal by the horn, and an hour after, "taps" sounds, when all are required to be in their quarters—and this, in endless repetition and without a variation, is the routine life of prison.

The Sanitary Commission, a benevolent association of exempts in aid of the Hospital Department of the Yankee army, published in July last, a "Narrative of Sufferings of United States Officers and Soldiers, Prisoners of War," in which a parallel is drawn, between the treatment of prisoners on both sides, greatly to the disadvantage of course, of "Dixie." Among other statements, in glorification of the humanity of the Great Republic, is one on page 80, from Miss Dix, the grand female dry nurse of Yankee Doodle, who by the by, gives unpardonable offence to the pulchritude of Yankeedom, by persistently *refusing to employ any but ugly women as nurses* —the vampire—which affirms that the prisoners at Point Lookout, "were supplied with vegetables, with the best of wheat bread, and fresh and salt meat three times daily in abundant measure."

Common gallantry forbids the characterization of this remarkable extract in harsher terms than to say that it is untrue *in every particular.*

It is quite likely that some Yankee official at Point Lookout, made this statement to the benevolent itinerant, and her only fault may be in suppressing the fact that she "*was informed,*" &c., &c. But it is altogether inexcusable in the Sanitary Commission, to attempt to palm such a falsehood upon the world, knowing its falsity, as they must. For my part, I never saw any one get enough of any thing to eat at Point Lookout, except the soup, and a tea spoonful of that was *too much* for ordinary digestion.

These digestive discomforts are greatly enhanced by the villainous character of the water, which is so impregnated with some mineral as to offend every nose, and induce diarrhœa in almost every alimentary canal. It colors every thing black in which it is allowed to rest, and a scum rises on the top of a vessel if it is left standing during the night, which reflects the prismatic colors as distinctly as the surface of a stagnant pool. Several examinations of this water have been made by chemical analysis, and they have uniformly resulted in its condemnation by scientific men, but the advantages of the position to the Yankees, so greatly counterbalance any claim of humanity, that Point Lookout is likely to remain a prison camp until the end of the war, especially as there are wells outside of "the Pen," which are not liable to these charges, the water of which is indeed perfectly pure and wholesome, so that the Yanks suffer no damage therefrom. I was not surprised therefore on my return to the Point, after three months absence, to find many preparations looking to the permanent occupancy of the place. It has already served the purposes of a prison, since the 25th of July, 1863, when the Gettysburg prisoners, or a large portion of them, were sent thither from the "Old Capitol," Fort McHenry and Fort Delaware, and the chances are that it will play the part of a jail until the period of the promised redemption of our National Currency.

Another local inconvenience is, the exposed location of the post. Situated on a low tongue of land jutting out into the bay, and, as I have before remarked, but a few inches above ordinary high tide, it is visited in winter by blasts whose severity has caused the death of several of the well-clad sentinels, even, altho' during the severest portion of the winter of 1863-4, they were relieved every thirty minutes—two hours being the usual time of guard duty. And when a strong easterly gale prevails for many hours in winter, a large portion of the camp is flooded by the sea, which finds convenient access by means of ditches constructed for the drainage of camp. When this calamity befalls the men, their case is pitiable indeed. The supply of wood issued to the prisoners during the winter was not enough to keep up the most moderate fires for two hours out of the twenty-four, and the only possible way of avoiding freezing, was by unremitting devotion to the blankets. This, however, became impossible when everything was afloat, and I was not surprised, therefore, to hear some pitiable tales of suffering during the past winter from this cause.

This latter evil might be somewhat mitigated but for a barbarous regulation peculiar, I believe, to this "pen," under which the Yanks stole from us any bed clothing we might possess, *beyond one blanket!* This petty larceny was effected through an instrumentality they call *inspections*. Once in every ten days an inspection is ordered, when all the prisoners turn out in their respective divisions and companies *in marching order*. They range themselves in long lines between the rows of tents, with their blankets and haversacks—those being the only articles considered orthodox possessions of a rebel. A Yankee inspects each man, taking away his extra blanket, if he has one, and appropriating any other superfluity he may chance to possess, and this accomplished, he visits the tents and seizes everything therein that under the convenient nomenclature of the Federals, is catalogued as "contraband,"—blankets, boots, hats, anything. The only way to avoid this, is by a judicious use of greenbacks,—and a trifle will suffice—it being true, with a few honorable exceptions, of course, that Yankee soldiers are very much like ships: to move them, you must "slush the ways."

In the matter of clothing, the management at Point Lookout is simply infamous. You can receive nothing in the way of clothing without giving up the corresponding article which you may chance to possess; and so rigid is this regulation, that men who come there bare-footed have been compelled to beg or buy a pair of worn out shoes to carry to the office in lieu of a pair sent them by their friends, before they could receive the latter. To what end this plundering is committed I could never ascertain, nor was I ever able to hear any better, or indeed any other reason advanced for it than that the possession of extra clothing would enable the prisoners to bribe their guards! Heaven help the virtue that a pair of second-hand Confederate breeches could seduce!

As I have mentioned the guards, and as this is a mosaic chapter, I may as well speak here as elsewhere of the method by which order is kept in camp. During the day the platform around the pen is constantly paced by sentinels chiefly of the Invalid (or, as it is now called, the Veteran Reserve) Corps, whose duty it is to see that the prisoners are orderly, and particularly, that no one crosses "the dead line." This is a shallow ditch traced around within the enclosure, about fifteen feet from the fence. The penalty for stepping over this is death, and although the sentinels are probably instructed to warn any one who may be violating the rule, the order does not seem to be imperative, and the negroes, when on duty, rarely troubled themselves with this superfluous formality. These were on duty during my stay at the Point, every third day, and their insolence and brutality were intolerable.

Besides this detail of day guard, which of course is preserved during the night, a patrol makes the rounds constantly from "taps," the last *horn* at night, to "reveille." These are usually armed with pistols for greater convenience, and as they are shielded from scrutiny by the darkness, the indignities and cruelties they oftentimes inflict on prisoners, who for any cause may be out of their tents between those hours, especially when the patrol are black, are outrageous. Many of these are of a character which could not by any periphrase be decently expressed,—they are, however, precisely the acts which a set of vulgar brutes, suddenly invested with irresponsible authority, might be expected to take delight in, and, as it is of course impossible to recognize them, redress is unattainable, ever. if one could brook the sneer and insult which would inevitably follow complaint. Indeed, most of the Yankees do not disguise their delight at the insolence of these Congoes.

CHAPTER VIII.

Houses Plebeian and Patrician—Love's Labor Lost—The Manufactures of Camp—Samples of Curious Workmanship—Washerwomen and Gamblers—Exceptional Prisoners.

I have said that the only shelter supplied by the Yankee government to the prisoners at Point Lookout is canvass. Tents are issued to the prisoners at the rate of one "A tent"—covering about six feet square—to each squad of *five*, or one Sibley tent—covering a circle whose diameter is about fifteen feet—to every eighteen men. The camp uniformity is however agreeably diversified by mansions of aristocratic proportions and finish, which from their material are styled "cracker-box houses." Top-boots and a cracker-box house fill the measure of any genuine Point Lookouter's ambition. To want these is to be the subject of envy—to possess them is to be its object, (I speak Kant—as many a better man before me.) It is only as a very special favor that a rebel is allowed to wear boots there at all, but the other blessing being attainable by all by means of a little cash, and much diligence, is a lawful object of universal ambition. They are made on this wise:

A large proportion of the bread used at all prisons consists of square crackers made of flour, water and salt alone, and thoroughly baked, which are put up in fifty pound boxes, and everywhere denominated "hard tack." The boxes in which these crackers are packed, are made of white pine or some other light and easily worked wood, and are, I suppose, about thirty-two inches long, by twenty broad and twelve deep. They are the perquisites of the prison Commissary, who sells them at from ten to fifteen cents apiece according to the demand. These are knocked to pieces carefully, the nails all saved, and the boards put away, until longer pieces of wood in sufficent numbers to make a frame are procured from outside. This accomplished, and the boards nailed on carefully, the "A tent" is slit up the back, and stretched across the ridge pole of the new domicile to form the roof. If newspapers, especially illustrated ones, can be procured, the walls are papered inside, increasing the comfort as well as bettering the appearance of the room—a fire place is made in the end, of sun-dried bricks of home manufacture, which having been raised four or five feet, is surmounted by a flour barrel; the floor is spread with sand from the beach, a table and a couple of chairs are improvised, bunks constructed, a name painted (with a composition of soot and vinegar) over the door; and the family moves in—men of mark and consequence forever henceforth in the chronicles of Point Lookout!

Most of these buildings have been put up by Marylanders, whose proximity to their homes enables them to command a larger exchequer than the other prisoners.

Many of the names by which these mansions are designated are purely fanciful, as "Here's your Mule," "The Alhambra," &c., but sometimes they are quite significant. I noticed a very neat one at the end of the division in which I slept, labelled "Home Again," and on enquiry learned that the appropriateness of the title depended on the following incident. It was erected on the ground of a former structure of the same kind, tenanted by the same parties, which came to grief as follows: Its occupants, an ingenious party with considerable mechanical skill, had contrived to accumulate cracker-box lumber in large quantities without exciting suspicion, and by watching their opportunities, had fashioned their material into two canoes, each capable of containing two or three men. These boats could be carried under the arm, the various parts disjointed, without exciting suspicion, and could be readily fitted together, even in the dark, by those who were familiar with their construction. Everything promised success, and they were awaiting a night of favoring darkness, having made the necessary arrangements for getting outside of the enclosure, (which it would not be prudent perhaps to disclose, as *that gate is still open,*) when the Yanks were somehow made acquainted with the scheme. They sent a guard to the house, found the canoes, made a bon-fire of them, and then razed the castle to the ground, leaving not a bit of it standing, "from turret to foundation stone." For some time the baffled tenants wandered around, pensioners upon the charity of their comrades; but at last they ventured on rebuilding their palace, and having accomplished this unmolested, they gave modest vent to their satisfaction as well as a visiting card to their friends, by writing over their door, "Home Again."

As I have spoken of the architectural ingenuity of the "rebs," I may as well do scant justice, here as elsewhere, to the surprising ingenuity and skill displayed by them in the various devices, with which they contrive to beguile the tedium (and buy the tobacco) of prison life.

The larger portion of the manufactures of the prisoners consists of rings, chains, breast-pins, shirt buttons, lockets, &c., of gutta percha. These are beautifully carved in an infinite diversity of style and design, and inlaid with gold, silver and pearl, in an endless variety of ornamental device. The rings are chiefly made of coat buttons; the chains exclusively I believe from a certain long hollow tube of gutta percha, used as a needle in some description of knitting or crochet, by sawing the cylinder into rings, slitting one side of each and thus linking them together; and the other ornaments are made principally of what is known as block gutta percha, the masses of which being of greater thickness, afford the means of heavier work. A large needle, to drill the holes for the pins, which confine the inlaid material, a hand lathe which can be made in a half hour, and a knife, one blade of which has been filed into a saw, are the only instruments required for this manufacture, though many who have been long at the business, have supplied themselves with graver's tool of every variety.

A more ambitious class of workmen confine themselves to carving in bone, and I remember a "Greek Slave," a "Paul in chains," and a "crucifix," by one of these which would not shame an experienced artist, and yet the maker had never carved a pipe, even, until he was a prisoner. I feel no hesitation in mentioning the name of the ingenious gentleman who wrought thus beautifully, nor any delicacy in giving this public expression to the hope that Mr. W. W. Marstellar,* will do himself and his native state, Virginia, the justice to cherish and mature the talent he so obviously possesses in unusual degree.

While these are the regular occupations of camp, no division is without one or two shoe-makers, and as many tailors, and barbers, who contrive somehow to obtain both the tools and materials of their trades, while here and there throughout the camp, you will find, ginger-bread and molasses candy of domestic manufacture for sale, and, strangely enough, one or two regular eating-houses, where a very respectable dinner can be obtained for fifty cents! The solvent power of money triumphs over every obstacle. Well and wisely wrote that rollicking son of Venusium :

"——————————————— rem facias : rem
Si possis recte, si non, quocunque modo rem."

Before my arrival at Point Lookout, two of its most celebrated pieces of workmanship had been sold outside. One of these was a locomotive, with a camp kettle for a boiler, and the other a watch, which filled a common canteen! both of which worked admirably, as I learned from many who inspected them. The handsomest and, considering all the difficulties, the most surprising, sample of mere mechanical ingenuity which I saw, was a violin made of a cracker-box, wherein all the curves and undulations of that præter-naturally twisted instrument were reproduced with the utmost fidelity. This curiosity stood the crucial test of practice, for I had the pleasure of hearing as honest a jig, extracted from its sonorous

---

*Mr. Marstellar presented one of the samples of his skill " Paul," through the hands of his former Colonel and Brigadier, our gallant Governor, *who never forgets his soldiers*, to General Lee, shortly after his return from prison and received a handsome autograph aknowledgement from the General.

body as ever tried the endurance or evidenced the skill of dame or demoiselle in all the tide of time.

Another source of extensive profits in prison is the pursuit of the washerwomen—if that phrase may be used without compromising the conscript liability of the subjects. The labors of these useful *ouvriers* are conducted on the beach at low tide. The beating of the waves against the bank, which is formed just here of a tenacious clay, leaves a little bluff some two or three feet high, along the bay face of the prison, which, as I have before mentioned, is free to the prisoners during the day. Here the washers most do congregate. Their first duty is to make a stove. This is effected by digging a round hole in this clay bluff, about eight inches in diameter, and as many deep, the outer rim of which is some four or five inches from the edge of the bluff. A second hole is then tunnelled in the face of the bluff, at such a distance below the surface as will allow it to strike the bottom of the first hole, so that the two apertures have the general form of the elbow of a stove pipe—and the furnace is complete. A fire is made in the larger cavity over the mouth of which the boiler is placed, being raised from the ground by a few pebbles that the draught may be perfect. The washerwoman rolls up his pants and wades out a few yards to clear water, fills his bucket with the salt tide, and is soon under weigh.

The washerwomen do not, however, monopolize this belt of ground, unfortunately. Its most numerous occupants are *gamblers*, who, under hastily constructed booths which they erect every morning and sleep on every night, carry on every game of cards at which money is staked, from aristocratic "faro" to cut-throat *monte*. Here the dice rattle and the cards are shuffled from morning till night, everything representing value, from a "hard tack" up, being freely offered and accepted as legitimate currency. In truth, the "hard tack" may be considered the unit of value in prison. One of them will purchase a single chew of tobacco anywhere in camp, eight will buy a U. S. postage stamp; ten a loaf of bread, &c. Indeed, the air resounds from rosy morn to dewy eve with such sounds as "Here's yer tobaccer for yer hard tack," "Here's envelopes for yer hard tack," and the like There is quite an amount of this commodity always in circulation, from the fact that many of the prisoners are not dependant on the government rations; so they draw their supplies and either give them or sell them to less fortunate neighbors, who in turn dispose of them to others more needy than themselves, so that the commerce of the "pen" consists in various exchanges, whose design and effect is to get hard tack from full mouths to empty ones.

Whence comes the money for all this gambling you naturally ask, and I confess I was for a long time puzzled by the phenomenon. The regulations of this prison not only prescribe, that all money shall be taken from prisoners on their entry, but that under no circumstances shall money be delivered to them. When friends, therefore, transmit them supplies of this sort, they are taken possession of by the commandant of the camp, who notifies the prisoner, and the latter is then permitted, in one form or another, to draw on the deposite thus made. At Point Lookout, under the *regime* at the time of our capture, the money was issued in sutler's checks or tickets, which the sutler was forbidden to receive again from any one not a prisoner. Subsequently, the plan was devised of handing to each prisoner who had money to his credit, a *pass-book*, on the first page of which he found himself credited with the money sent him, and debited with the cost of the book, and by taking this account book to the sutler, purchases could be effected to the amount of the balance due. But, under whatever form, *money obtained, by some means, admission.* Rebel ingenuity managed it, and I am overwhelmed with regret, oh, most indulgent of readers, that "the exigencies of the public service" do not permit me to say *how.* I know you are not satisfied, but "odds bodikins!" how can I help that? Curiosity has brought many a man and woman to condign grief since our common grandmother's unfortunate *escapade*, and, doubtless, will continue to be the vestibule to misery till the crack of doom. Ruminate thereon, and be comforted, for tell you, I am resolved beyond hope of repentance, I will not.

As this is a chapter devoted somewhat to the rarities of prisondom, I must not forget to mention that among the convicts is a woman! She was captured in the Valley of Virginia, I was informed, while acting as a member of an artillery company, and her sex discovered, probably, on the usual search for valuables. Common civility suggested a conversation with her, and one day as I was passing the little tent, which was assigned to her exclusively, I approached her for the purpose of making some inquiries, as well as letting her know that we were disposed to serve her in any way possible to prisoners. She seemed, however, indisposed to converse and I was compelled to give up the chase. Why the Yanks detain her, I can't imagine, as I believe in the rare instances in which these Amazonian propensities have brought the sex to trouble, heretofore, on either side, their exchange has been promptly made.

Another "*rara avis*"—the remainder of the line is even more pointedly appropriate—is a genuine "Old Virginny" negro, named "Dick," whilom a servant at the Bollingbrook Hotel, in Petersburg, who was taken while in the service as cook to some mess, during the Gettysburg campaign. Dick has been importuned, time and again, to renounce the Confederate cause, come out of prison and accept work and good wages outside, but he resists with Roman fortitude—protests that he is a "Jeff. Davis" man, that he is going back to his home, and wants nothing to do with the Yankees, and expresses the most appropriate and sovereign contempt for "Old Abe." It is positively exhilarating to see such loyal devotion in a slave, tempted and persecuted by the enemy as they are, and it involves many sacrifices, besides the usual ones of prison, to stand his ground so manfully. Chief among these, probably, is the jeers of his fellow-negroes when on duty. But Dick rises sublimely superior to all this, and quietly pursues his labors with no more apparent annoyances or regrets, than are supposed to be inseparable from the pursuits of any other overworked washerwoman—that being his profession.

The advent of the Petersburg delegation was a source of mingled mortification and delight to him. He obviously regretted to see us in bonds, but he was glad to hear news of many who had been dead to him for a year, and his gratification took the practical turn of placing his purse and labor at our disposal.

Day now followed day in tedious progression, little occurring to break the monotony of a life which has all the stupidity of a tread-mill without its exercise. The few incidents that marked it, I cannot, perhaps, more conveniently dispose of than by extracting from my diary, with a little amplification for greater clearness.

CHAPTER IX.

A Negro Raid—Major Weymouth—General Augur Inspects Us—Fall of Petersburg—Camp Inspection—Petersburg in Mourning—Letter from Home—Culottes and Sans-Culottes—Speculations Alimentary.

Thursday, June 16th. A prisoner a week to-day—it seems a year. Last night the negro regiment which constitutes part of our guard, and which has been raiding over in Westmoreland and the adjacent counties, returned with great beating of drums and blowing of fifes. The captives of these brave soldiers of the Republic, consisted of a hundred head of cattle, principally poor women's cows, several plows, buggies, primeval sulkies, harrows, beds, chairs, &c., and from twenty to thirty decrepit citizens! This is the service in which these demons are regularly employed. Every month, and sometimes more frequently than once in thirty days, they are sent across the river on a plundering tour. The Yankees are too much ashamed of this, to fill their papers with the doings of these valiant "swash bucklers," but they are glad of the means of keeping alive by this promise of stated plunderings, the *martial ardor* and *fidelity* of their black brethren, and of course, are not unwilling to *share the spoils.* These raids, which are usually made in a country entirely devoid of Confederate soldiers, are, of course, without any earthly justification or purpose, except to gratify the malignity and feed the beastliness of their new allies, whose delight in these safe robberies is, as may be expected, boundless. The old men are usually kept a short time in an unenclosed camp outside, under guard of the negroes, and then returned to their homes, the Yankees even not having the audacity to detain them—perhaps not the humanity to feed them.

Saw to-day, for the first time, the Chief Provost Marshal, Major H. G. O. Weymouth. He is a handsome official with ruddy face, a rather frank countenance, and a cork-leg. He conducts this establishment on the "*laissez faire*" principle—in short he lets it alone severely. Whatever the abuses or complaints, or reforms, the only way to reach him is by communications through official channels, said channels being usually the authors of the abuses! It may be easily computed how many documents of this description would be likely to reach him.

Two or three times a week he rides into camp with a sturdy knave behind him, at a respectful distance—makes the run of one or two streets and is gone, and I presume sits down over a glass of brandy and water, and indites a most satisfactory report of the condition of the "rebs," for the perusal of his superior officer, or plies some credulous spinster with specious fictions about the comfort, abundance and general desirableness of Yankee prisons. Major bears a bad reputation here, in the matter of money—all of which I presume arises from the unreasonableness of the "rebs," who are not aware that they have no rights, which Yankees are bound to respect.

Friday, June 17th.—A salute of thirteen guns heralded

this morning, the arrival of General Augur, who commands the department of Washington. About 12 m., the general with a few other officials, made the tour of camp, performing in the prevailing perfunctory manner the official duty of inspection.

Wandered about among my fellow-prisoners to-day, and found nearly all of the new comers suffering from the poisonous water.

Sunday, June 19th.—The New York papers received to-day are blatant with accounts, most detailed and circumstantial of the capture of Petersburg. The back door of Richmond is now secured say the editors, and bets are freely offered in Grant's army, according to the correspondents, that the "Fourth of July" will be celebrated under the shadow of Washington's statue, on Capitol Square in Richmond! All this I believe with unhesitating faith to be a lie of the first water, explicable alone in the light of the circumstance, that *the regular mail for Europe left yesterday.* Such of General Grant's officers as celebrate the "Fourth" in Richmond, will perform that patriotic service in the Libby, and to-morrow's papers, (the steamer being gone,) will contradict the falsehood of to-day. And yet—and here's the psychological paradox in the matter—the credulous Yanks, though thus deceived on a moderate calculation, three hundred and sixty five times in every year of grace since the war began, are as ready now to be deluded as in the earliest hour of the earliest day, and the enterprising geniuses who control, or furnish news for, the press of the North, play the game of wholesale lying, with the same profound audacity and superb success this blessed day, as when they first gave American circulation to the European simile "lying like a bulletin." Mein Gott vot a beebles!

To-day, we were blessed with our first practical experience of the beauties of a Yankee inspection. The massacre of the innocent (blankets) was wholesale and very provoking. I performed an acceptable service for a fellow-prisoner, by appearing in line with his extra blanket in my hand, not having one of my own. Our division being a new one—for though sleeping in the fourth, I answered roll in the twelfth—the prisoners had but little superfluous cloth of any sort, and the Yank who did the stealing from us, was obviously mortified at the scant game he bagged.

While waiting dutifully, hour by hour, for our inspector to approach and perform his task, the gates of the prison opened and a batch of "rebs," numbering a couple of hundred entered. Among them were several of our fellow-citizens of Petersburg, captured in the attack of the preceding Thursday I believe, by Baldy Smith and Hancock, which gave rise to the flaming particulars of the capture of the gallant Cockade, so ostentatiously displayed in the journals of Saturday. They assure us that our little city is still safe, but the accounts they bring of the distress of the inhabitants, on the day after our capture are heart-rending. I can well imagine it. Only a drop, it was, truly, in that fierce tide, each refluent wave of which comes to the shore of the South, crested with the shattered wrecks of the best and dearest, and noblest of her sons, yet to those mourning homes in Petersburg, shuddering with the agony of an unexpected and bloody woe, that drop was a consuming flood. Her young men had gone into the war, with a noble prodigality of their lives, and health, and comfort, that proved them worthy of the ancient fame of their little city, and of the priceless heritage they coveted, and when they fell they were mourned indeed, but it was a sacrifice anticipated and in some sort prepared for. But on that day, the fathers and grand-fathers fell—the bullet cheated the grave. The blood-stained locks were grey—the pallid cheeks were *wrinkled*. It was not mothers that wailed the lost, but daughters and daughter's daughters! Yet, how well and worthily these heroes shed their blood, let the record of the villainies now staining, as I write, the track of Sherman, attest!

Tuesday, June 21st.—As I expected, the capture of Petersburg was a mere Yankee lie, which having accomplished its purpose, be the same financial or political, is now shelved as quietly as the same versatile people sacrifice a principle, or decapitate a general when either has served their turn.

The further issue of cracker-boxes to the prisoners was prohibited to-day, so that an elegant arrangement by which I proposed in company with five or six others, to become a P. L. aristocrat is postponed, if not prevented utterly. As our rulers do not vouchsafe any excuse for this act, we are of course left to conjecture as to the cause, and guesses at the motives of the conduct of these worthies are not likely to prove signally profitable.

Io triumphe! I received to-day a letter! To ordinary mortal eyes this may seem, nothing more than a common quadrangle of M. S., distinguished by the *imprimatur* of a certain official outside the "pen," who stamps our correspondence "Prisoner's Letter, Examined," but to me, hungering and thirsting after news of home, this was as grateful as the first golden distillation of the grape to our pluvious progenitor in the earliest autumn after the Deluge. (N. B. This simile is copyrighted.) The regulations of all the prisons prohibit prisoners, from sending or receiving a longer letter than one page. At Point Lookout the ellipsis which may be supposed to follow the word "page," in the "general order," is filled with the words "of note paper." So that one had to acquire a telegraphic habit of writing or be content to say little. Some geniuses whose fancies refused this mathematical curb, were in the habit of writing their letters at the usual length, and cutting them off by the page and sending them "by detail," very much as ships are built "Down East" by the mile, and then cut off to suit purchasers:—while others cultivated a microscopic penmanship, which must be eminently useful to them on their return to Dixie, unless paper falls in the market meanwhile.

Tuesday, June 21st. On the prison bulletin board—an institution by which general information is conveyed to prisoners—a list was pasted this morning, containing the names of parties for whom there were boxes or packages to deliver, and to my considerable joy, my name appeared in the list.

These presents to, or purchases by prisoners, are delivered at a door in the South side of the enclosure, which opens through the fence and into an office or store room, where the packages are received, opened, examined, and all that escapes the regulations (and the *regulators*) turned over to the owners. As before remarked, this performance is conducted on the most ascetic principles as respects clothing, no one being allowed to take any articles of outside wear, from hat to shoes, (boots are *mala prohibita*,) unless he deposites the corresponding article of his existing stock. It becomes necessary, therefore, if one has any article of apparel, that he is not exactly prepared to turn over to his merciful masters, to find some method of evading the laws. This was not very difficult. All that was necessary, was to buy or beg or "flank" a suit of clothes, to surrender which would involve no other sacrifice than that purely emotional one which founds our attachment to certain things, on account of an absurd veneration for antiquity. Accordingly, I beat up quarters for a half an hour, till I *accumulated* a suit that would have entitled me to an exalted position among the raggedest vagrants in Naples or Constantinople. My shoes had to be coaxed to stay on, by an arrangement after the fashion of a surcingle, which strapped them to my feet. My hat only deserved the name from the circumstance that in some mythical era of the past, it was attached to certain others, and *relatively very extensive* portions of organized matter, now, alas, long resolved into their original elements,—the combination of which constituted the article in question, though I am free to say, it would have required the anatomical intuition of a Cuvier, to have deduced the *castor* from the specimen. It being a warm summer day, I conceived it would excite no suspicion to appear without a coat, so my only other article of external costume, was one, which with great and many misgivings, I venture to enter on the catalogue of pantaloons. Verily, verily, never since the martial ancestors of the gay Parisians invented these indispensable institutions of dress, (and I have Gibbon's authority for the assertion, that they *deserve* that credit,) did such a travesty on costume, disgust the eye of taste. Innocent of buttons, both legs out at the knees, stained by time and less tender agencies out of all approach to its original color, with an enormous quadrilateral, carved out of it in a location which indeed could best spare so large a tax, but which modesty forbids me to make particular reference to, it was only by a diligent and scientific application of pins, that I could induce it to preserve even a bifurcate appearance, while the assistance of one hand was necessary to keep the entire compilation from demolition, and the wearer from the miserable fate of Parson Adams, in his celebrated nocturnal encounter in the inn. Long ere this, oh, most comical of costumes, thou hast found appropriate service in the terrifying of crows, or more noble fate, "the paper mill hath claimed thee for its own."

Thus caparisoned, however, and assuming an air of such desolation as might be considered appropriate to preserve the *tout ensemble*, I wended my way to the office. As I passed along, my ragganuffin appearance excited, of course, a little comment, which I bore with philantrophic patience till one villainous "reb," presuming on the position of the hand that was doing the duty of a pair of suspenders, suggested with a solemn wag of his head, "maybe a little Jamaiky ginger might help yer, mister!"

To the office I went, however, but my preparations turned out to be all in vain. My package consisted of a beef tongue and a can of "solidified cream." I returned to my quarters with my plunder, gave myself a denuding shake, which reduced my dress pretty much to the condition of the memorable "one horse shay," and summoning my mess-mates, soon forgot both the troubles and the farce of costuming in diligent application to the "provant." Oh, Dalgetty, prince and prototype of the military Bohemian, with what wisdom and justice did you assign the highest place in the soldier's scale to "rations."

It is quite humiliating to those whose idea of the superior

dignity of humanity is so very exalted, to confess how much of the good and evil, great and little, objective as well as subjective, of life is dependant on the average dinner a man gets, but the fact is indisputable. I claim no originality for this reflection. Forty years ago Byron wrote

"——————————all human history attests
That happiness for man—the hungry sinner—
Since Eve ate apples, much depends on dinner."

And whoever troubles his brain with the unfashionable labor of thinking, will be apt to conclude with me, that much besides happiness hangs on the same thread. What is the reason that the Romans conquered the world? Merely this—they were generous feeders. Who can account for the fact that the hardy Scotsman has not been able to hold his own against his less stalwart neighbor below the Tweed, except as a result of the fact that oat meal, though flanked by usquebaugh, is no match for wheat flour with only beer for an ally? Why have the Indians so steadily and so extensively bowed their necks before the English? Preachers, and philanthropists, and editors, and place-men, all have their ready-made theories to account for the phenomenon, but the patent fact, which they won't confess, because it don't suit their hypotheses, is that Nana Saib ate *rice*, but Havelock *roast beef*. Why was Cassius a conspirator? Because he was "lean and hungry." Why did Napoleon lose Waterloo? Merely because he was too fat, as he confesses. Why wont revolution succeed in Ireland? Depend upon it, the root of the mischief is the potato. Who could be humane on raw beef or virtuous on truffles?

Shakespeare recognized the general connection in his broad assertion "Fat paunches have lean pates," and many a long century before him, the candid Horace, regardless of the danger he ran of having his criticism turned on his jolly rotund little self, uttered the same thought.

"Pingue pecus domino facias, et cetera, *præter,
Ingenium.*"

Indeed, I am not sure that those philosophers were wholly

in the wrong who located the soul in the stomach, and being an optimist I find great comfort in the thought that if this be true, few will be lost for want of attention to this tabernacle of the nobler part of man.

CHAPTER X.

Officers Leaving—Effect of Yankee Insults—Fourth Division in Trouble—Cabinet Making—Negro Exodus—A new Prison—The Fourth—Maryland and Marylanders.

Thursday, June 23rd. The officers who were confined in a pen near us, were to-day removed, preparatory to sending them to Fort Delaware. It has been determined to keep no commissioned prisoners at this point. To-day, the negroes are again on guard, and are very insolent. Like all the rest of these sable patriots, they seem to have exhausted the resources of darkness to form their complexions, and their conduct is as black as their skin. There is however a compensation in all this—it is exhilarating to witness the effect on the prisoners—how it deepens and widens the gulf between them and the canting crew, who seek such agencies to make imprisonment torture. The truth is, it is everywhere apparent throughout the history of this conflict, that all that is necessary to crystallize into unsolvable hate, the lingering lukewarmness of a Southern man or community, whose faint hearts go out hungering after the Egyptian flesh-pots, is to bring them face to face with the enemy. The cruelty, blood-thirstiness, avarice, hypocrisy, vulgar despotism and brutality, which characterize so many of our enemies, need only to be once seen, and above all once *felt*, to summon every Southron to the altar, that he may take the Carthaginian oath of undying **hate** to his enemies. And hence it is, that wherever the fortune of war has set the foot of a Yankee General in command of Yankee troops, there is to be found the most unyielding, uncompromising fealty to the patriot cause, and the most inextinguishable hate to the Yankees. Our stupid foes imagine that the desolation and ruin, which they everywhere dispense, terrify the hostile and re-assure the wavering, and that these Christian arguments will not fail to produce conviction wherever strongly presented. But they are as ignorant as they are depraved—such treatment has never subdued a free people in all the tide of time. The dragon teeth they sow, spring up behind them an army of mailed men. The whirlwind comes of the sown wind—and out of the ashes of ruined homesteads, forth from the bosom of the scourged earth, out of the agony of dying men, and the worse than dying women is born the fierce insatiate cry for vengeance, and the unconquerable resolution to be free. And similar in kind is the result of the insults deliberately and purposely inflicted on prisoners.

An order was issued to us to-day, prohibiting the lighting of any more fires in camp, so that the extra cooking, which we have been able to give our half raw rations is foreclosed. Hoping to be able to perform this important, if not necessary service to my "salt horse" to-day, I went out on the beach and was lighting a fire there, when one of the ebony custodians ordered "dat fire out d—n quick," and I ate half-raw meat perforce. Before night-fall our Yankee sergeant visited the various tents in our Division and "confiscated" the lightwood, we had purchased and stored away as fuel. It was a trifling matter unquestionably, but the air of satisfaction with which this worthy "clothed in a little brief authority," performed his task, gave to each motion of the vulgarian the sting of a personal affront.

The members of the Fourth Division came to exceeding grief to-day. Some of the tin cans in which our slops are furnished, were missing from the tables of that division after breakfast, and when the "rebs" of that section marched up for their dinner, they were quietly told, to expect no rations till the missing cups were found. The Edinburg Review rose according to Sydney Smith, by "stress of politics," and I suppose the return of the missing tin-ware may be coerced by stress of starvation. At all events the Fourth Division "rebs" must test the efficacy of the system through much alimentary tribulation.

I find I am becoming Sybaritic, and though a crumpled rose leaf might not interfere fatally with my sleep, the planks on the floor of my kind host's house certainly do. This morning, therefore, I conceived a French bedstead—this evening it is *un fait accompli*. An empty flour barrel and two poles about six and a half feet long, constituted my stock. I knocked the barrel to pieces and nailed the staves on the poles, placed about two feet apart and parallel. Then nailing over the hoops which I had straitened out for the purpose, I had a comfortable springy bedstead, which in the day-time, I shall place on its end at the back of the ranche out of the way, and in the night time extend at length, between the bunks with which our house is already supplied. This is the cheapest and best of improvised bedsteads, and I commend it to gentlemen of expensive tastes who may be similarly circumstanced.

The boys are laughing at the summons which S., one of my fellow Petersburgers got to-day, from a negro sentinel. S. had on when captured, and I suppose still possesses, a tall beaver of the antique pattern, considered inseparable from extreme respectability in the last decade, and for many a year before. While wandering around the enclosure, seeking I suspect "*what* he might devour," he accidentally stepped beyond "the dead line," and was suddenly arrested by a summons from the nearest negro on the parapet, who seemed to be in doubt whether so well dressed a man could be a "reb," and therefore whether he should be shot at once.

"White man, you b'long in dar?"

"Yes."

"Well aint you got no better sense den to cross dat line?"

"I did not notice the line."

"Well you better notice it, an' dat quick or I'll blow half dat *nail kag* off?"

It is needless to say, that the owner of the "nail kag," "stood not upon the order of his going."

Friday, July 1st. To-day, one of the negro regiments that has been guarding us—the 36th U. S. Colored—left this point for the front, their places being taken by another black regiment ordered here, it is said, by Butler for cowardice in presence of the enemy, (good joke for Butler,) and the 5th Massachusetts Colored Cavalry. Negro-like, the out-going regiment left singing, in a most orthodox plantation whine, the National (African) Anthem, "John Brown's body lies mouldering in the ground."

One of the disgraced (!) darkies was standing near me as the regiment passed our gates with every jaw extended, and with a knowing wag of the head, he observed "Niggers is such fools. Dey is gwine away wid der moufs open, but dey'll came back wid 'em shot, I 'speck." On they travelled making the welkin ring with

"John Brown's body lies a mouldering in the ground,
John Brown's body lies a mouldering in the ground,
John Brown's body lies a mouldering in the ground,
But his soul is a marching on."

All of which and much more of the same sort was chanted with that monotonous cadence that many a time and oft we have all heard at camp-meetings and corn-shuckings, under the inspiring influence of religion in the one, and—*horresco referens*—rot-gut in the other. It was not many weeks before their mangled bodies were clogging up that horrible valley of death, which the fatal mining of Grant clove in a certain memorable hill-side of Petersburg, where for nearly an hour, at short grape range, the cannoniers of the Army of Northern Virginia, dealt destruction from their safe embrasures upon the writhing, powerless and baffled columns of assault.

Saturday, July 2nd. A notice was posted on the public bulletin board to-day, requiring all prisoners who were brought from Belle Plain, on the 23rd of May, to fall in at the gate, at 9 a. m. This is preparatory to a move somewhere, and the rumor is that Elmira, N. Y., is to be the point of destination. I hope our turn will not be long coming, or this infernal water will settle the question of exchange as far as regards me personally, in a very unsatisfactory manner. I am not at all superstitious in the matter of sepulture, but, if I have an antipathy thereanent, it is to being buried at Point Lookout. I hardly think the example of Wellington in the old world, or Webster in the new, both of whom died by the sea, could reconcile me to such a fate just now.

Monday, July 4th. This is the day that all America was wont to dedicate to lemonade, ice cream, pic-nics and patriotism. I remember well one "Fourth," so long back that I decline to enter into any vulgar arithmetic about it, when, in obedience to a custom almost as universal as that sanguinary Indian rule which denies the privileges of the tribe to a young man until he scalps an enemy, I, who write to you, assumed the *toga virilis* by means of a Fourth of July oration, and worked myself into a perspiration, and my amiable auditory into demonstrative gratification over the glories and greatness, the prowess and the perpetuity of the Union ! And here am I, this blessed day of grace, suffering condign pains and penalties at the hands of the successor of Washington, for the———but, hang politics, I made a vow twenty days ago that, unless mightily moved by some Yankee, I would eschew all thought of politics until I saw my own good flag once more, and as you have done me no particular harm that I wot of, most courteous reader, I'll spare you. Suffice it to say, that Point Lookout, July 4th, 1864, and Petersburg, July 4th, 18—, were about as different dates in all their relations to the writer, as any two points of time could well be. On the latter occasion, I enjoyed various exhilarations, which now in the retrospect refuse to arrange themselves in any regularity or method, but present a confused melange of ice cream, Declaration of Independence, sherry-cobbler, military procession, national salute, fruit cake, toasts, orator of the day, excessively wet shirt collar, millions of fans,—I wont *qualify* as to the number,—pretty women, (mainly from the country!) congratulations and an immense dinner—admire the climax! But the other date ushered in divers miseries, and nothing but hard tack and fat pork! Verily, verily, Plautus is right, "The gods have us men for foot-balls."

All this and much more of the same sort, which I charitably spare you, ran through my mind as I took my usual morning promenade on the beach to-day, and watched the streamers and flags spreading from main-top to bow-sprit over the wicked looking gunboat that watched (and showed its teeth, for that matter) like a naval Cerberus over the gates of our "pen." At 12, M., the stars and stripes were flung out, and the national salute of thirty-I-do-not-know-how-many guns fired, amid the piping and drumming and braying of Yankee Doodle, from divers bands ashore and aboard. The "rebs" had no idea, however, of permitting the Yanks to monopolize the fun, and on a couple of the patrician mansions of "cracker-box row," there might be seen diminutive copies of our own Southern Cross, gaily flung out "to the bold breeze of heaven," after the manner detailed in one of the many metrical villainies which have been palmed off on the long suffering Southern people, under the name of National Anthems, any time these four years back.

I noticed particularly on the "Home Again" house a pretty Confederate flag, which must either have been manufactured inside, or conveyed very surreptitiously from the outside by some ingenious sympathiser – a *woman* " for a ducat"—who had the courage to dare, and the wit to baffle Yankee jealousy of everything suggestive of the "so called." This house was occupied, and if it stands, I suppose still is, by Marylanders, and I will not have a better opportunity than this to challenge for these exiles from that noble state, a reversal of the unjust reproach which has been cast upon her from various quarters, and in various forms in the South. It is doubtless true, that there are cowards and knaves in Maryland, and it is not less true that every Southern State and Northern, could furnish many a sample to place by the side of those who have earned so much reproach for her. But it is quite as true that no people in any part of the world have furnished more illustrious examples of pure, unselfish, uncompromising, all sacrificing devotion than now distinguishes the citizens of that gallant State. I knew much of this before. I had seen her brave sons suffering a long and bitter exile from all that was dear to them—uncheered by hope of speedy return—cut off from their families—hurled, in many cases, from affluence to poverty—condemned to the disheartening spectacle of witnessing their possessions enjoyed, their friends imprisoned, their state controlled by an abhorred race, imported from New England to colonize and *convert* Maryland. And yet, I had seen them gallantly bearing a banner which no hand of ours has been able to maintain on any spot of Maryland's soil for thirty days, hoping against hope while the weary years rolled on for the day of deliverance, and faltering not, nor failing, though their hearts sank in the pain and palsy of that hope forever deferred. So have I seen her fair daughters, many of them tenderly and delicately raised, forced to choose exile as the alternative of a jail—perchance for some act of common humanity to a Confederate soldier—or voluntarily embracing the perils and hardships, because in their generous, loyal hearts, approving the principles, and sympathising with the sufferings of our beleaguered Confederacy, spending their days near the hospital cot, and devoting their nights to the toils of the busy needle, for an army that has never yet been strong enough, to give them an escort for one short day to their hospitable city of monuments. All this have I seen, and have seen it oftentimes repeated, and I have placed it to the credit of that noble State against the recreancy of the few Marylanders who have skulked among us, and the many *not Marylanders*, who have counterfeited the name to cloak their cowardice. But it was not till I became a prisoner that I appreciated to the full the devotion of her children. When I saw them cheerfully enduring the privations of a long imprisonment, almost within sight of their own homes, many of them persecuted with solicitations from their nearest relatives to come out, take the oath, and enjoy every comfort that wealth and society can offer, all of them conscious that a word would unlock the prison gates and send them forth to their families, with no one to question or reproach them; and then learned of the many hundreds of Marylanders at various periods who were tenants of that pen, some of whom are prisoners of over a year's standing, *not five in all* had taken the oath of allegiance to the Yankee government, I felt that the best of us might take a lesson from their patriotic constancy. And when a few months afterwards, I saw some of these very men marched like felons through their own fair city, without permission to whisper a word—scarcely to cast a look at mothers and sisters standing by, who were heart-hungry for the poor privilege of a mere greeting, and yet saw no cheek blanch, no muscle quiver, no weakening of their proud resolve to fight the fight out for principle, through every sacrifice and every peril—calmly, nay, with a smile on their lips, half of triumph, half of scorn, answering the taunts of their keepers—they marching from prison to exile while I was marching from prison to my home, I felt as I now feel the wish that the Confederacy was peopled with such men. Let not their names nor their deeds die—let some pen meet for the task, gather now while the events are fresh, the memorials of her children in this war for freedom where they have so little to hope—so much to fear, and though the fortune of war should separate them and the Confederacy from their beloved State, let history do justice to the faithful living, and let a nation's gratitude lay immortal laurels o'er

"the sacred grave
Of the last few who, vainly brave,
Die for the land they cannot save."

CHAPTER XI.

More Prisoners Leaving—Sinking of the Alabama—Miss Gilbert's Career—Sutler's Tricks—Water getting Scarce—Going Out on Detail—Off for Elmira.

Tuesday, July 5th. Another batch of prisoners, those who arrived here on the 8th of June, received a summons yesterday to be in readiness to leave, and were carried out of camp. As we were the next tenants to these in the order of time, I presume we will be next called.

Two items of news are furnished us by the papers to-day—one the anticipation of a raid by Early into Maryland—the other, the destruction of the *Alabama* by the *Kearsage.* Fortunately the two came together, so we managed to endure the latter with some composure, though both surprised and mortified that Semmes should have lost his ship, and the Confederacy his invaluable services, for a time at least, on a point of professional etiquette. Still it may be said of most naval as well as of most other duels, that the result is purely an accident. The exploding or failure to explode of a particular shell—an event utterly beyond the skill or control of any one aboard, may, and in this instance did, constitute the whole matter. No one suggests a doubt of the courage and coolness with which Semmes pursued his chivalric resolve, and the result might well have been anticipated, aside from the intervention of chance, when we reflect that one vessel was a merchantman in fact, as far as regards its pursuits, with a crew of common sailors with but one battle experience, while the other was a man-of-war with a crew trained especially and exclusively for this description of duty. And yet the Yankees themselves admit that if a certain shell that penetrated their stern had exploded, Messrs. Winslow & Co. would have been very thankful to the *Greyhound* for any such little favors as were subsequently extended to the Confederates ; while the French account adds that Capt. Semmes endeavored from the first to discard the element of accident from the fight, by getting to close quarters, and settling the question in a fair, stand up, hand to hand encounter—a manœuvre that the Yank had no stomach for, and successfully used his superior sailing qualities to avoid. Still it is a great victory for Doodledom, and no higher compliment could be paid the *Alabama* and her gallant company, than is furnished in the extravagant joy of our enemies over the loss of the "great pirate." The "old flag" may again perchance steal up to the "top" of the boasted merchant marine, a half a million tons of which the dreaded "pirate" drove from the seas in six months! The hundreds of pious frauds whereby nominal transfers of Boston and New York bottoms were made to English and French owners, so that the "Yanks" might pocket the receipts without taking the risks of the carrying trade, will now be repented of and renounced—said frauds being no longer profitable. Commodore Vanderbilt may make the run from Panama without a convoy, and Cape Cod may fish in peace.

Meanwhile the Suabians in the Quaker State are hurrying off their beeves and blinding their horses,* and General Wallace is putting Baltimore in a state of defence, an operation that seems "always doing, never done."

Started to-day on a literary hunt and fished up from the recesses of one of the cook-houses a promising looking volume arrayed in all the attractive gorgeousness of faultless typography and binding, and entitled "Miss Gilbert's Career." The title page announces that it was the 20th thousand, a circumstance I can only explain, in common justice to Yankee taste, by supposing that the 20th thousand was printed before the first ditto.

---

*This perfectly original barbarity was committed time and again on the occasion of General Lee's entry into Pennsylvania, in June, 1863. Rather than take the trouble to remove these horses, they would blind the poor brutes by puncturing their eyes with a needle, thus making them useless to us for army purposes, while their value as draft animals, or for farm uses was not very largely impaired. In many cases we found the poor beasts with their eyes still overflowing with tears and blood, from the merciless hands of their masters.

Such a common place vulgarity as Miss Gilbert, I undertake to say, never could have been produced on any soil of earth other than "Massachusetts Bay and Providence Plantations." There are situations, however, wherein anything in print is endurable, and I waded, with the patience of a professional proof-reader, through every sentence and syllable of the dreary platitudes of Miss Gilbert. I record this incident solely as a contribution to the next edition of Abercrombie on the Mind, since it establishes beyond cavil the enormous *vis inertiæ* of the human intellect, and I commend the book to all those who believe that the brain, like the muscles, can be strengthened by subjection to unusual and repeated strains. Dr. Windship, the modern Hercules, boasts that he can raise 3600 pounds—a capacity he has acquired by constant effort in that direction, and I have no doubt that equal diligence in the mental line would ensure results equally marvellous. If any one wishes to try the experiment, I recommend mental calisthenics with a pair of such books as the aforesaid "Career," as I consider it about as heavy as the stout doctor's dumb-bells, (the source of all his marvellous strength,) which weigh as much as a flour barrel apiece.

Wednesday, July 6th. More rumors. Grant, say the correspondents, has demanded the surrender of Petersburg. *Peut-être!* Early is playing the wild with the Baltimore and Ohio railroad, and, greatest grief of all *to us*, the sutler informs us that the further sale of articles of food to us will be suspended, as the authorities are informed that our sutlers are prohibited from selling such things to their prisoners. On hearing this announcement, I made my moan to the first acquaintance I met, who happened to be an old prisoner. He greatly calmed my fears by assuring me that this was an old dodge designed *to bring in rapidly the sutler's checks in order to the entire disposal of the stock on hand*, which was probably larger than he desired to keep this hot weather. This was very reassuring, as I had just received notice that there was a "money letter" in the Major's hands for me, whose advent and use I anticipated with much watering of the mouth.

The ruse of course succeeded, and the sutler's "powerful"

butter, game herrings, animated cheese, and sour meal, began to disappear with a celerity that must have been very satisfactory to him, if not to the deluded Confederates, who were thus seduced into an unusual quantity of purchases.

Oh Yank, Yank, how art thou Yankeefied?

Thursday, July 7th. The supply of water is getting very scant, and the quality very infamous. Guards have been placed over some of the pumps to prevent waste, and these being "negroes," it is necessary, in order to get a drop, to ask permission in respectful terms of the sable sentinels who, to do them justice, do not seem disposed to abuse their position. I attribute this to the circumstance that these are negroes, who have been in service, and any soldier will tell you, that an active campaign is very humanizing. With every precaution the amount is still so insufficient that a water-boat, had to be sent down from Baltimore to-day, to furnish a supply to the hospitals, and a detail has been engaged most of the morning, wheeling in barrels of it for the use of the sick.

There is quite a contention for the privilege of working in this as on other details, there being some privileges attached thereto. Almost every day there is some description of labor to be performed outside of the pen, for which volunteers are sought and easily obtained among the prisoners. Those selected for the work are mustered into a company, their names taken down, and under Yankee guards they are carried outside to the scene of their work. This consists principally in the unloading of vessels at the wharf, in building hospitals, commissary store-rooms, stables, &c., &c. The legitimate benefits of these details are, first, occupation, second, a little liberty, third, the chance to hear some news, and fourth, a small piece of tobacco. The semi-legitimate benefits are, the gathering up of refuse pieces of plank, old iron, nails and the like, which command a high price (in tobacco or hard tack,) within the "pen." The illegitimate, and I fear the most operative inducement with some of the unregenerate "rebs," is the opportunity of pilfering along the wharf and among the vessels whose cargoes they are discharging, which the nature of their duties frequently affords. From one cause or another —generally, I suppose, from a combination of several, the detail list is always full, and places thereon command a premium.

In the earlier periods of Point Lookout history, there was an additional advantage in these details, inasmuch as the opportunity of escape was thereby frequently afforded and embraced, but the multiplication of the precautions which experience of "rebel" ingenuity occasioned, has rendered the blockade for several months past pretty effectual.

Friday, July 8th. No newspapers permitted to be brought into camp to-day. Early is doubtless frightening Father Abe prodigiously, and he fears the stimulating effect, on his misguided enemies in prison. The weather has been furiously hot for a week past, and as the earth is a sparkling sand, and everything about us is a glaring white, many besides myself are suffering with inflamed eyes,—a chronic disorder here.

Saturday, July 9th. To-day is the first mensiversary of my imprisonment. Any super-fastidious reader who objects to my word-coinage, is hereby informed, that he is at perfect liberty to draw his pencil through the obnoxious polysyllable and substitute therefor any word, or form of words, that will better please him, but I hold it, nevertheless, to be a perfectly defensible creation.

At 10 this morning, the prisoners who arrived on the 14th of June, of whom we were a part, were summoned before the gate and in a short time we had gathered our few "traps," had made our adieu to the friends who were to be left behind, and having been formed into line and counted, we were marched into the officer's pen, now empty. A couple of hours afterwards, we were ordered to the Provost Marshal's office where we were divided into companies, muster-rolls made out, and under a strong guard of the V. R. Corps, we were carried to the wharf which was the scene of our exceeding discomfort a few weeks before, and at 1 p. m., were stowed away, about three hundred of us, aboard a crazy craft, rejoicing in the sounding title "El Cid." Down the ladder, into a reeking hold where the heat and stench would have overpowered any other animal than a Confederate prisoner, we trooped along, packing ourselves away in the fashion which the mellifluous Wilberforce was so fond of expatiating on, under the name of " the horrors of the middle passage," until the last " Southern Confederate " crossed the taffrail, the gang-plank was drawn in, and at 2 p. m., we turned our backs on Point Lookout, we hoped forever.

"*O wer weis, &c.*" you'll find the rest in Schiller's Don Carlos, but lest the great German play may not be at hand, I recall a good, if true, translation in Robby Burns' proverb,

"The best laid schemes of mice an' men
Aft gang agley."

CHAPTER XII.

Marine Moralizings—" El Cid "—A Disagreeable Passage —Gliding Up the Narrows—A Good Samaritan—New York —Aboard the Cars—Secesh Sympathizers—Elmira.

The man who first invented going to sea was *hostis humani generis*, a super-eminent donkey, and should have been outlawed accordingly. The element is proverbially treacherous, the dangers are great, the inconveniences infinite, the results moonshine, and to crown all, beneficent Nature has implanted in every human stomach an instinctive and vigorous protest against the practice, which ought to satisfy any reasonable being, that it never was designed that a creature innocent of fins, tail or a shell, should go out of sight of land. I admit, that the whale oil supply was for a long time an obstacle to the general acceptance of my view of the case, but the vast fields of petroleum recently discovered, knocks the wind out of that argument and allows me to indulge the reasonable hope, that before "my eyes turn to behold for the last time the sun in heaven;" I shall have the satisfaction of participating in a general auction of all marine properties, "on account of whom it may concern."

The fact is, there is nothing redeeming about the infernal sea-going system. You get up in the morning and there is no newspaper; you stroll out to settle your bitters and a dozen paces in any direction will introduce you to a shark; you stagger in to breakfast, and the coffee slides into your beef steak, and both into your lap; you get up, and in ten minutes you discover in the language of the luckless yellow-plush, "wot tin basins was made for;" the day passes and there is no post office, no business, no counting room, no children run over, no street cries, no omnibus, no dog fight, no civilization, it snows and you cant go sleighing, it is fair and you cant take a drive, it rains and you cant roll ten-pins, or get satisfactorily drunk; pale spectres with pendant jaws and watery eyes, all by a strange centrifugal force, flying towards the outside of the ship, pass you at every instant, and after a day dismally dragged through in every conceivable discomfort, you turn in at night to a closet not large enough to swing a cat in, and tumble into a berth which looks so much like a coffin, that you dream before you are well asleep of attending your own funeral!

So your days creep along, if you have vitality enough to survive, destitute of fox hunts or flirtations, law or literature, politics or opera, fashion plates or scandal, telegrams or taxes, and if the old scythe-bearer comes to your relief, you are sewed up in a sack with a thirty-two pound shot at your heels, and tossed to the fishes as remorselessly as the beef bones from yesterday's soup!

Gonzalo was a very Solomon: "Now," he cries, and I whenever aboard ship, with him,

"Now would I give a thousand furlongs of sea for an acre of barren ground: long heath, brown furze, anything: the wills above be done, but I would fain die a dry death."

All these objections are sound and unexaggerated, if you are a first class passenger aboard a first class steamer. "Phancy our feelinx," then when you remember that we were packed like sheep on a cattle train, in the hold of a villainous tub in the middle of July, with no ventilation, except what was afforded by two narrow hatchways, (there being no side lights,) and permission to put our heads above the deck being only accorded to two at a time, and then for five minutes, so that it required one hundred and fity times five minutes, or over half the day to elapse before you could get your second gasp of fresh air! And then our ship was such a crazy and unseaworthy craft, that in the event of a storm, there was little prospect of our ever seeing land again except on the hypothesis of Pisanio that

"*Fortune* brings in some boats that are not steered."

In this delightful situation, the sun melting the pitch in the seams over our heads, and not air enough stirring to raise a ripple, we stretched ourselves on the lower deck in a desperate state of disgust, with only energy enough to pray for a short passage or a heavy gale—blessings craved in vain. Anything short of a wheel-barrow ought to make the run from Point Lookout to New York—our destination—in thirty hours or thirty-five at the most; it took us just forty-six, although the sea was as calm as a river, nothing breaking the smoothness of its treacherous surface, except that infernal stomach-pump contrivance, known as the "ground swell,"—a submarine wave which constantly beats from the shore, and was intended by beneficent nature to prevent her children from the folly of navigation, by circling the whole ocean with this (unheeded) warning against leaving land. From 10 a. m., Saturday the 9th, until we arrived in New York harbor, a period of over fifty hours, our only food was one ration of bread and a small piece of fat pork, and what with this and a slight dose of sea-sickness, I was consummately miserable by the time we got into "the Narrows" early Monday morning. I stole up on deck, and hunting up the officer commanding the guard, asked permission to purchase a cup of coffee from the cook, and leave also to remain on deck till I could drink it. He assented readily, and having made the contract with the presiding genius of the galley, I took my seat on a "bit" forward, and drank my fill of the beautiful scene around me. Those who have entered New York harbor by this channel—and what southron has not, in those days when Gotham was our Ostium and Piraeus?—will remember the richness and luxury of the Jersey coast for thirty miles below the city. The land is high, handsomely wooded, and almost every summit is crowned with a stylish country villa—the urban residences of the princes of Wall street and Broadway, while in every reach of shore where a surf breaks, a handsome hotel fronts the sea, and rows of piquant little cottages dot the hill slopes to their tops. As you approach the city, these evidences of wealth and taste increase in number and in magnificence, and you are ushered into the teeming port of the American Venice, through a highway of palaces, with here and there a powerful fortress interspersed, to give security to all this rural luxury and elegance.

I was musing on all this, indulging my taste for the beautiful, but amazingly hungry and uncomfortable withal, when a Yankee corporal, a German Jew, named Bernstein, as I afterwards learned, came to where I sat, with a smoking cup of coffee in his hand, his own ration for breakfast, and with a courteous apology for having nothing better to offer, insisted on my drinking it. It was idle to tell him that I had engaged to get some from the cook, for he replied, that the cook might not have it to give me, and on my objecting that he would lose his own breakfast, he assured me that he could get another cup, and would be offended if I did not take it. So I accepted it very gratefully. Not all the sherbets that ever Persian poets sung, not Byron's memorable thimble-full of essence frozen out of a bottle of champagne, not "Lachryma Christi," beloved of Sue, not Perkins' "best pale" to a Briton, nor Schwartz's imperial "lager" to a Bavarian, nor poteen to a Wexford man, nor usquebaugh to a Highlander, nor train-oil to a Laplander, nor spermaceti candles to the late Czar, could have matched in refreshment that half pint of black coffee to me.

"I greet it now, I gulped it then."

There is no likelihood that these lines will ever meet his eye, but I could wish that such might be their fate, that my friend Bernstein might see that his little act of kindness is not and will not be forgotten. Before I had finished, he hunted up his haversack and laid before me as many "hard tacks" as I could eat, so that when, a half an hour afterwards, the cook told me he had a breakfast for me, I was able to administer alimentary consolation to a couple of hungry "rebs" below.

It was near mid-day when we hauled up in the channel just off and below the Jersey city end of the lower ferry to New York, and there we lay till the train on the Erie railroad, whose eastern terminus is here, was ready. I am quite familiar with New York harbor, and many a spire of the city was as easily recognized as that of my Virginia home. Everything seemed as busy, as "alive," as stirring, as in the same month, four years before, when I last saw the gay city. The war was apparently little felt here. The docks were as crowded, the same unvarying hum filled the sultry air, the ferry boats passed with the same surcharged loads, the wharves were crowded with the same rushing hordes of porters, hackmen, stevedores, news-boys and thieves, and I doubt not Broadway echoed to the same endless tide of wheel and foot, and Wall street choked its crooked throat with as excited and thronging a congregation as have ever "bulled and beared" it in the shadow of old Trinity, on any July day this quarter of a century past. In the face of all this wealth, development, material power—all these vast appliances of conquest, I felt a new pride in our beleaguered Confederacy, which has had nothing to oppose to this unexampled affluence of resource except the unconquerable gallantry of her children, and yet has fought this fight against such odds as have never yet stood in the way of Freedom, with a calm confidence in the cause, a noble acceptance of sacrifice, an undaunted courage, a patient hope, a chivalric devotion, that fearlessly challenge the comparisons of history.

A little boat is shooting out from shore, and in a moment more an officer boards us, who probably brings news that the train is now waiting, for our "tub" is now turned towards the dock. We are soon along side, an officer stands at the hatchway to count us as we come up, lest some may conceal themselves in the ship. The count seems satisfactory, for we are marched into the depot, a few paces off, and put aboard a train of box and passenger cars, standing ready for us.

Our advent is unexpected, or the Jerseyans are not as curious as their compatriots elsewhere, for there is but a small crowd of spectators, and these gaze on us with a stolid air, which may mean sympathy; probably, however, indifference. By half past one all was in readiness, the locomotive gave that preliminary shriek, which, according to Sydney Smith, is most like the scream an attorney may be expected to give when the devil gets hold of him, and off we started for Elmira.

The Erie railroad, as I presume, every one *used to* know, runs through the northern counties of New Jersey, and the southern counties of central and western New York. It passes through some handsome towns and cities, but the country is considered far inferior to that which lines the Central road. At almost every station, we made a lengthy halt, to give way to some regular train passing up or down, and, wherever we stopped, we were the subjects of very great, and, generally, respectful interest. The guards rigidly excluded the people from all intercourse with us, and forbade, under various sanguinary threats, any assistance being tendered us, still they found it impossible to guard every avenue of approach, and many a piece of tobacco, package of crackers, and the like, was handed us by the good people on the route. The gentler sex was conspicuous in these charities, and more than once surprised us by furtive exhibitions of little Confederate flags which they had concealed about their persons. At one point, there seemed to be a fair prospect of a difficulty between our guards and the citizens, many of whom persisted, despite all orders, in making such contributions to our wants as accidentally lay in their power. Of course, these agreeable incidents were occasionally diversified by the insults of some sleek non-combatant, whose valiant soul found congenial occupation in fearful threats of our indiscriminate massacre, if he could only lay hands on us. These gentry were, in the main, of that physical and sartorial type which we always associate with the idea of extreme orthodoxy—your sanctimonious, high-seat-in-the-synagogue worthies, who

"Compound for sins they are inclined to,
By damning those they have no mind to,"

and from the serene heights of their sublime self-conceit, hurl worse anathemas than that *prolix* profanity of bishop Ernulphus, at the forlorn publicans below. You know the canting breed, good reader mine, wherever you see them, and at home or abroad, in pulpit or tribune, in church or state, they everywhere exhibit the same harmonious blending of Heap's hypocricy with the villainy of Carker. Of these lovely lambs, Butler is the god and Kalloch the prophet. He would be a most unreasonable "reb" who would look for anything but a snarl from these curs.

And thus, amid friends and foes, through gorges and around bluffs, now skimming gaily along a level meadow, and anon "wiring in and wiring out," apparently in the absurd effort to avoid crossing the Susquehannah—a stream so crooked that the engineers who built the road seem to have fancied, that, by following up one bank, they would, sooner or later, find themselves on the other—on we steamed till about 8 o'clock, Tuesday morning, when we pulled up in the pretty little city of Elmira, on the left bank of the Chemung, and, although about to enter our prison, a much happier party than when we left "El Cid." This being the last time I shall have occasion to mention this miraculous sample of naval architecture, I here deliberately devote it to the infernal gods, with as honest an unction as ever filled the bosom of the most patriotic Moor, in the times of its great namesake—a gentleman who must have served Moorish mothers with impracticable cherubs a good turn—he frightened the grown ones so prodigiously, according to the authentic histories of Bob Southey, and that unfortunate victim of a liver complaint, and an uncongenial spouse, Mrs. Hemans.

CHAPTER XIII.

Statistics—Formation of a Prison Camp at Elmira—Our Entrance—Arrangement of The Pen—Major Henry V. Colt—Clerical and Executive Officers—A Precious Trio—Number of Prisoners.

I plainly foresee that this chapter is going to run into statistics, and as I have had a reasonable horror of mathematics from the blessed days when my nose had to be held whenever the medicine chest required depletion, and every application of my mind to figures was followed by the application to my shoulders of something else, I will be excused for invoking the patience of the reader, assuring him—a favorite lie with flagellatory parents while "horsing" their heirs—that the pain I inflict causes me more suffering than it can possibly occasion him.

For more than a year before our arrival, Elmira was the site of the rendezvous for the drafted men of western New York. Here the gushing patriots were received and housed, trained to turn out their toes and survive "hard tack," and otherwise qualified to patch the rents in a certain lacerated Anaconda, which has been prowling around the cotton and tobacco country with varying fortunes these four years back. These gay volunteers required three camps, which were severally denominated "barracks" 1, 2 and 3, and here they were kept till they graduated in the manual of arms, and squandered their bounty money, when they were incontinently bundled off to the front, a performance which, according to most authentic averments, resulted in the absconding of about 25 per cent. of the patriots before they ever came in sight of a camp sample of "the old flag."

Now it came to pass, that Mr. Stanton began to feel some apprehension that the "secesh" were getting too numerous at

Point Lookout, and offered too tempting a prize to the profane general, then menacing the sour-krout and smear-case (?) of the honest Deutschers in rural Pennsylvania, so he ordained and established by imperial ukase a prison in the hyperborean regions of New York, where for at least four months of every year, anything short of a polar-bear would find locomotion impracticable, and where, therefore, no apprehension need be be felt of trouble within, or assault without, for the same interval. Early in July, therefore, the "Yanks" were ousted from Barrcks No. 3, and preparations made for receiving the first instalment of prisoners, who arrived on the 6th of July, numbering three hundred and ninety-nine, the four hundreth man having escaped on the way. On the 11th, two hundred and forty-nine arrived, and the next day we were added to the list.

We were escorted to the "pen," by a large concourse of admiring citizens, a number of whom were of the gentler sex, in every stage of development, curiosity being *in Elmira*, a failing of the sex. A march of about a mile, brought us to our prison. We filed in, were counted, divided into companies of a hundred, the roll called, and we were led off to our quarters. These consisted of wooden buildings, about one hundred feet long, by sixteen in width, and high enough for two rows of bunks. There were about thirty-five of these buildings in the enclosure, standing side by side, in a line parallel to the front of the pen, and about mid way the ground. I soon asserted a pre-emption claim to a top bunk, and having deposited my very modest "pack," started out to view my premises.

I found a level plain of about thirty acres of land, situated as I have said, a mile or so west of Elmira, and immediately on the bank of the Chemung. The ground is unequally divided by a long narrow lake or lagoon, which runs parallel to the river, into two sections, the one farthest from the entrance gate, being denominated the Trans-Mississippi Department, in the vernacular of camp. This lake starts within twenty feet of the fence on one side of the pen, and flows under the opposite fence, and the ground beyond the lake is a sandy bottom, indicating what I found on enquiry to be the case, that the unruly Chemung occasionally gets uproarious, overflows its banks and floods the adjacent grounds.

The whole site is a basin surrounded by hills which rise several hundred feet, and are covered richly and thickly with the luxurious foliage of the hemlock, ash, poplar, and pine. This was the most grateful relief from our Point Lookout experience, where nothing met the eye, in any direction except the sky, water, and prison fence. But a more available and practical improvement was in the water, which was here pure, cool, and abundant, and the new comers luxuriated in the delicious beverage with the gusto of a lost traveller in Sahara, or a repentant legislator after a nocturnal spree.

In the general arrangement of the guard detail there was little difference from Point Lookout, except in the *absence* of the colored guards, and in the *presence* of the officers, all of whom spent a portion of each day within the "pen." A row of tents running parallel with the front fence of the "pen," was assigned to these gentry, and until the approach of winter drove them into certain barracks outside, where ventilating arrangements were not so extensive, they continued to occupy them.

Back of the 34 or 35 barracks, already referred to, is a row of wooden buildings, containing the adjutant's office, dispensary, various rooms of Yankee sergeants, store-rooms, and the like, and back again of these, the mess-rooms and cook-houses, which extend to the lagoon. These, with one or two other buildings, constituted all the appliances of the prison at that time, nor was any change made until the miasma from the lagoon sowed the seeds of febrile disease so widely, that eight or ten hospitals had to be built, and the advent of prisoners by the thousand, exhausted the sleeping capacity of the barracks.

The government of this prison was, and is still, in the hands of Major Henry V. Colt, 104th, N. Y. Volunteers, a gentleman about 38 years of age, five and a half feet high, with a florid complexion, a comfortable *embonpoint*, a very prepossessing appearance and manner, and a chronic attack of cigar-smoking. I perform a very grateful duty in here bearing testimony to the various admirable qualities of this gentleman as an officer and a man. Uniformly urbane and courteous in his demeanor, he discharged the varied, and often times annoying, offices of his post, with a degree of justice to his position and to the men under his charge, a patience, fidelity and humanity, that could not be surpassed, and, I fancy, are seldom equalled, either side of the line, in similar positions. There was none of the slip-shod indifference of Point Lookout *regime*. Major Colt either discharged in person, or superintended the execution of every duty respecting the prison, which appropriately claimed his attention, doing all with the thoroughness of a trained man of business, and although charged with duties, whose performance demanded almost every moment of his time, he was always ready to hear and redress any just complaints that were made to him, or to afford any information or assistance, consistently with his position, to the humblest prisoner. It is a pleasant office to do this justice to an enemy, and to record this offset to the many cruelties which are charged, no doubt justly, to other officers in charge of our unfortunate prisoners.

The Major's adjutant was Captain C. C. Barton, an active, smart, and rather consequential young gentleman, as adjutants are wont to be—and here I call attention to the fact that these officers constitute a class, *sui generis*, in every army—but, upon the whole, Barton was a good fellow, notwithstanding he considered Abe Lincoln a gentleman, and accounted Grant a compound in about equal proportions of King Solomon and Alexander the Great. Captain B. was assisted by a young sergeant named Hopkins, who was promoted to an adjutant's place shortly after our arrival, but did not exchange his comfortable quarters for "the front" till the summer was over; and a youth, named Frank Earle, who, in a fit of spasmodic patriotism, joined a heavy artillery company, before he was out of his teens, and straightway perilled his invaluable life for his beloved country, as an adjutant's clerk, in the dangerous "Department of the Chemung."

In the executive duties of his office, Major Colt was assisted by fifteen or twenty officers, and as many non-commissioned officers, chiefly of the militia or the veteran reserves. Among them were some characters which are worth a paragraph.

There was a long-nosed, long-faced, long-jawed, long-bearded, long-bodied, long-legged, endless-footed, and long-skirted curiosity, yclept Captain Peck, ostensibly engaged in taking charge of certain companies of "rebs," but really employed in turning a penny by huckstering the various products of prisoners' skill—an occupation very profitable to Peck, but generally unsatisfactory, in a pecuniary way, to the "rebs." Many of them have told me of the impossibility of getting their just dues from the prying, round-shouldered captain, who had a snarl and an oath for every one out of whom he was not, at that instant, making money, and exhibited generally the characteristics of a long ancestry of Connecticut clock peddlers. He diversified his speculations in cheap jewelry, by attentions to a handsome mare, of which he seemed quite proud, and who was far the nobler animal I suspect.

Another rarity of the "pen" was one Lieut. Jno. McConnell, a "braw chiel," who had eclipsed fiction in his noble deeds while in the field, and whose bile was so grievously stirred up against the rebels that he could not keep his tongue or hands from them even here. He had an oath and a drawn pistol on every occasion, and would fly into a passion over the merest nothing, that would have been exceedingly amusing, but for a wicked habit he had of laying about him with a stick, a tent pole—anything that fell into his hands. He was opening a trench one day, through the camp, when, for the crime of stepping across it, he forced a poor, sick boy, who was on his way to the dispensary for medicine, to leap backwards and forwards over it till he fell from exhaustion amid the voluble oaths of the valiant lieutenant. One lieutenant Richmond kept McC. in countenance by following closely his example. He is a little compound of fice and weasel, and having charge of the cleaning up of the camp, has abundant opportunities to bully and insult, but being, fortunately, very far short of grenadier size, he does not use his boot or fist as freely as his great exemplar, who is never idle. No one, however, was safe from either of them, who, however accidentally and innocently, fell in their way, physically or metaphorically.

Of the same block Captain Bowden was a chip: a fair-haired, light-moustached Saxon-faced "Yank"—far the worst type of man, let me tell you, yet discovered—whose whole intercourse with the prisoners was the essence of brutality. An illustration will paint him more thoroughly than a philippic. A prisoner named Hale, belonging to the old Stonewall brigade, was discovered one day rather less sober than was allowable to any but the loyal, and Bowden being officer of the guard, arrested him and demanded where he got his liquor. This he refused to tell, as it would compromise others, and any one but a Yankee would have put him in the guard house, compelled him to wear a barrel shirt, or inflicted some punishment *proportionate to his offence.* All this would have been very natural, but not Bowdenish; so this valorous Parolles determined to apply the torture to force a confession! Hale was accordingly tied up by the thumbs, that is, his thumbs were fastened securely together behind his back, and a rope being attached to the cord uniting them, it was passed over a cross bar over his head and hauled down until it raised the sufferer so nearly off the ground that the entire weight of his body was sustained by his thumbs, strained in an unnatural position, his toes merely touching the ground. The torture of this at the wrists and shoulder joints is exquisite, but Hale persisted in refusing, and called on his fellow-prisoners, many of whom were witnesses of this refined villainy, to remember this when they get home. Bowden grew exasperated at his victim's fortitude, and determined to gag him. This he essayed to accomplish by fastening a heavy oak tent-pin in his mouth, and when he would not open his mouth sufficiently—not an easy operation—he struck him in the face with the oaken billet, a blow which broke several of his teeth and covered his mouth with blood!

On the other hand, some of the officers were as humane and merciful as these wretches were brutal and cowardly, and all who were my fellow-prisoners, will recall, with grateful remembrance, Captain Benj. Munger, Lieutenant Dalgleish, Sergeant-major Rudd, Lieutenant McRee, Lieutenant Haggerty, commissary of one of the regiments guarding us, a whole-souled fellow, and one or two others.

These officers were assigned in the proportion of one to every company at first, but to every three-hundred or four-hundred men afterwards, and were charged with the duty of superintending roll-calls, inspecting quarters, and seeing that the men under their charge got their rations, and *the system* was excellent.

During the month of July, 4,323 prisoners were entered on the records of Elmira prison, and by the 29th of August, the date of the last arrivals, 9,607.

The barrack accommodations did not suffice for quite half of them, and the remainder were provided with "A" tents, in which they continued to be housed when I left the prison in the middle of the following October, although the weather was piercingly cold. Thinly clad as they came from a summer's campaign, many of them without blankets, and without even a handful of straw between them and the frozen earth, it will surprise no one that the suffering, even at that early day, was considerable.

CHAPTER XIV.

Medical—A Sage Doctor—Pride of Consistency—General Hospital Arrangements—Commissariat—The Rations and the Rats—Punishments.

As I have spoken of the military government of Elmira Prison, it may not be inappropriate to pursue the statistical view, now that I am in it, by a brief chapter on the Medical and Commissary Departments, before I resume the thread of the more personal portion of my narrative.

The head of the Medical Staff was Major E. L. Sanger, a gentleman who appeared very faithful, though not quite as industrious as the needs of such a post would seem to demand, in the discharge of the supervisory duties, especially falling under his charge. He was assisted by Dr. Rider, of Rochester, one of the few "Copperheads," whom I met in any office, great or small at the North. My association was rather more intimate with him than with any of the others, and I believe him to have been a competent and faithful officer. Personally I acknowledge his many kindnesses with gratitude. The rest of the "meds" were in truth, a motly crew in the main, most of them being selected from the impossibility, it would seem, of doing anything else with them. I remember one of the worthies, whose miraculous length of leg and neck, suggested "crane" to all observers, whose innocence of medicine was quite refreshing. On being sent for to prescribe for a prisoner, who was said to have bilious fever, he asked the druggist, a "reb," in the most *naive* manner, what was the usual treatment for that disease! Fortunately, during his stay at Elmira, which was not long, there were no drugs in the Dispensary, or I shudder to picture the consequences. This department was constantly undergoing changes, and I suspect that the whole system was intended as part of the education of the young doctors assigned to us, for as soon as they learned to distinguish between quinine and magnesia they were removed to another field of labor.

The whole camp was divided into wards, to which physicians were assigned, among whom were three "rebel" prisoners, Dr. Lynch of Baltimore, Dr. Martin of South Carolina, Dr. Graham, formerly of Stonewall Jackson's Staff, and a fellow townsman of the lamented hero. These ward physicians treated the simplest cases in their patient's Barrack, and transferred the more dangerous ones to the Hopitals, of which there were ten or twelve, capable of accommodating about eighty patients each. Here every arrangement was made that *carpenters* could make, to insure the patients against unnecessary mortality, and indeed a *system* was professed, which would have delighted the heart of a Sister of Charity, but, alas, the practice was quite another thing. The most scandalous neglect prevailed even in so simple a matter as providing food for the sick, and I do not doubt that many of those who died, perished from actual starvation. Sometimes the fault would be, that a lazy doctor would not make out his provision return in time, in which case his whole ward must go without food, or with an inadequate supply till the next day. Another time there would be a difficulty between the Chief Surgeon and the Commissary, whose general relations were of the stripe characterized by S. P. Andrews, as "cat-and-dogamy," which would result in the latter refusing to furnish the former with bread for the sick! In almost all cases the "*spiritus frumenti*" failed to get to the patients, or in so small a quantity after the various *tolls*, that it would not quicken the circulation of a canary. Another trouble was, the inexcusable deficiency of drugs. During several weeks in which Dysentery and Inflammation of the Bowels were the prevalent diseases in prison, there was not a grain of any preparation of opium in the Dispensary, and many a poor fellow died for the want of a common medicine, which no family is ordinarily without—that is if men ever die for want of drugs.

There would be and is much excuse for such deficiencies in the South, and this is a matter, which the Yankees studiously ignore—inasmuch as the blockade renders it impossible to procure any luxuries even for our own sick, and curtails and renders enormously expensive the supply of drugs, of the simplest kind, providing they are exotics; but in a nation whose boast it is that they do not feel the war, with the world open to them, and supplies of all sorts wonderfully abundant, it is simply infamous to starve the sick as they did there, and equally discreditable to deny them medicines—indispensable, according to Esculapian traditions. The result of the ignorance of the doctors, and of the sparseness of these supplies, was soon apparent in the shocking mortality of this camp, notwithstanding the healthfulness claimed for the situation. This exceeded even the reported mortality of Andersonville, great as that was, and disgraceful as it was to our government and to civilization, if it resulted from causes within the control of our authorities. A published report made to Lincoln, by four returned Andersonville prisoners alleged, that out of a population of about 36,000 at that pen, six thousand or *one sixth of the whole*, died between the 1st of February and the 1st of August, 1864. Now at Elmira, the quota was not made up till the last of August, so that September was the first month during which any just proportion could be taken, and out of less than 9,500 prisoners there at that time, 386 died during that month. The same rate of mortality for six months, would give 2316 or nearly *one fourth of the whole*. A deduction must be made, arising from the fact, that as the whole number decreased by deaths, so the deaths might be expected to decrease, but making every allowance, the mortality will appear to be as great in this model prison as in the worst "pen" in the South, and at Elmira it resulted, in the majority of cases, from causes that the government could have controlled. During the last six weeks of my prison life, it was my duty to make out the morning report of the deaths, so I speak by the card as to these matters. And apropos of this Death Record, two facts therein were quite remarkable; so much so that I called the attention of many to them; the first was the large number of North Carolinians who died, numbering generally nearly, if not quite half of the whole number—a fact I turn over to Mr. Gradgrind, "without note or comment;" the second, the entire absence of deaths from intermittent fever, or any similar complaint. Now, I knew well that many of the sick died from this and kindred diseases produced by the miasma of the stagnant lake in our camp, but the reports which I consolidated every morning, contained no reference to them. I enquired at the Dispensary, where the reports were first handed in the cause of this anomaly, and learned that Dr. Sanger would sign no report, which ascribed to any of these diseases, the death of the patient! I concluded that he must have committed himself to the harmlessness of the lagoon in question, and determined to preserve his consistency at the expense of our lives, very much after the fashion of that illustrious ornament of the profession, Dr. Sangrado, who continued his warm water and phlebotomy, merely because he had written a book in praise of that practice, although "in six weeks he made more widows and orphans than the siege of Troy."

I could hardly help visiting on Dr. Sanger the reproaches his predecessor received at the hands of the persecuted people of Valladolid, who "were sometimes very brutal in their grief," and called the Doctor and Gil Blas no more euphonious name than "ignorant assassins."

Any post in the Medical Department in a Yankee prison camp is quite valuable on account of the opportunities of plunder it affords, and many of the virtuous "meds" made extensive use of their advantages. Vast quantities of quinine were prescribed that were never taken—the price, eight dollars an ounce, tempting the cupidity of the physicians beyond all resistance, but the grand speculation was in whisky, which was supplied to the Dispensary in large quantities, and could be obtained for a consideration in any reasonable amount from a "steward" who pervaded that establishment.

The Commissary Department was under the charge of a cute, active ex-bank officer, Captain G. C. Whiton. The ration of bread was usually a full pound *per diem*, forty-five barrels of flour being converted daily into loaves in the bakeshop on the premises. The meat ration, on the other hand, was invariably scanty, and I learned on enquiry, that the fresh beef sent to the prison usually fell short from one thousand to twelve hundred pounds, in each consignment. The expedients resorted to by the men to supply this want of animal food were disgusting. Many found an acceptable substitute in rats, with which the place abounded, and these Chinese delicacies commanded an average price of about four cents apiece—in greenbacks. I have seen scores of them in various states of preparation, and have been assured by those who indulged in them, that worse things have been eaten—an estimate of their value that I took on trust.

Others found in the barrels of refuse fat, which were accumulated at the cook-house, and in the pickings of the bones, which were cut out of the meat and thrown out in a dirty heap back of the kitchen to be removed once a week, the means of satisfying the craving for meat, which rations would not satisfy. I have seen a mob of hungry "rebs," besiege the bone-cart, and beg from the driver fragments on which an August sun had been burning for several days, until the impenetrable nose of a Congo could hardly have endured them.

While on the subject of rations I may refer to a substance used very generally here in the preparation of soup, which adds greatly to its healthfulness and which, as I have not heard of it from prisoners elsewhere, is, I suppose, peculiar to this prison—dessicated vegetables. A couple of hundred pounds of the matter—which consisted of all kinds of vegetables, kiln-dried and compressed into cakes of about a foot square and two inches thick—would thicken soup for 9000 men, at a cost very insignificant.

Twice a day the camp poured its thousands into the mess rooms where each man's ration was assigned him, and twice a day the aforesaid rations were characterized by disappointed "rebs" in language not to be found in a prayer book. Those whose appetite was stronger than their apprehensions frequently contrived to supply their wants by "flanking"—a performance which consisted in joining two or more companies as they successively went to the mess-rooms, or in quietly sweeping up a ration as the company filed down the table.—As every ration so flanked was, however, obtained at the expense of some helpless fellow prisoner, who must lose that meal, the practice was almost universally frowned upon, and the criminal when discovered, as was frequently the case was subjected to instant punishment.

This was either confinement in the guard house, solitary confinement on bread and water, the "sweat box," or the barrel shirt. The war has made all these terms familiar, except the third perhaps: by it I mean a wooden box about seven feet high, twenty inches wide, and twelve deep, which was

placed on end in front of the Major's tent. Few could stand in this, without elevating the shoulders considerably, and when the door was fastened, all motion was out of the question. The prisoner had to stand with his limbs rigid and immovable, until the jailor opened the door, and it was far the most dreaded of the *peines fortes et dures* of the pen. In midsummer I can fancy that a couple of hours in such a coffin, would inspire Tartuffe himself with virtuous thoughts.

CHAPTER XV.

Historic Precedents—Adventures with the Doctor—Major Colt—My Duties—My Privileges—Promotion—Comrades.

When the illustrious Anne of Austria entered the city of Paris, with her son Louis the Fourteenth, a few words were spoken to her by the President de Bailleul, which, according to the account of "solitary horseman," James, changed the whole after history of France. So the Constitution of the United States, now considerably shattered by exposure in the trenches, sprang from no more dignified source than a canal project of that genuine Virginian, George Washington. So the fact that Charles I, of England, stammered, cost his Majesty his head. So certain architectural speculations of that bull-headed Hanoverian, George III, cost Britain the brightest jewel in her crown. So the absurd weakness of Louis le Jeune, for shaving his chin precipitated France into four centuries of warfare. In short, that venerable Romance, known by courtesy under the name of History, is crowded with illustrations about as veritable as anything else therein, of the fact that the most important of all matters may spring from causes the most absurdly insignificant.

I have not made these references, oh much-enduring reader of mine, to convict you of incorrigible ignorance in not having known them before, though that would be a laudable motive enough, no doubt; nor to make a learned exordium to Chapter XV, though that would be entirely justifiable, since such things have an air of extreme respectability, and sugar-coat an essay very much as a flaming caption in a New York newspaper carries off a whole litany of unimportant lies below. In good sooth, my only purpose was to claim credence for an averment I am about to make, by showing that my experience was not exceptional, and that there is nothing absolutely without a parallel, in the declaration, that I owe whatever of peculiar advantage I enjoyed, throughout my whole stay at Elmira, to a sudden attack of that undignified disorder which is treated with copious libations of extract of anise-seed, in infantile victims, and Jamaica ginger and paragoric when the patient gets well out of long clothes, but which the mature wisdom of adult age finds most certain relief from, in Otard or Hennessey "*straight*."

As Napoleon is said to have been a constant victim to this complaint, I need not blush to own that I was similarly afflicted on my arrival at Elmira, and soon wended my way to the drug store to seek a remedy. Such are the wiles of temperance people, that it will not do to ask, under such circumstances, for a dram: the subterfuges of the Maine Law men having destroyed human confidence to an alarming degree, so I suggested "ginger" to a mild-looking descendant—*longe intervalle*—of Esculapius, whom I found the presiding genius of the dispensary. I must have made my request in a super professional tone, for he straightway inquired whether I were a practitioner of medicine. Being among enemies, I exhibited none of the indignation proper to such an imputation, and commanding my feelings, merely returned a decided "no," but the doctor evidently doubted me still, and seemed to infer that I must needs have a diploma, because I knew the *quant. suf.* of Brown's Essence, so he insisted that I should consent to come and aid him in the daily augmenting duties of his new post. As, however, I did not have quite impudence enough to undertake the bolus business, I stoutly resisted, to the mingled amazement and grief of the chief Surgeon, and was about to leave with my dose, when the Doctor intimated that I might obtain employment at Headquarters by making application, whereupon, I framed, in immaculate caligraphy, a note to Major Colt, requesting him to assign me to some duty, which, without compromising my position as a hopeless "rebel," would give me employment—something to eke out the monotonous days of durance. This, the Doctor, in whose eyes I had evidently found favor—I do not suppose he *meant* an insult by suspecting me of medicine—undertook to deliver.

Night soon came, and on a French bedstead, composed of a couple of planks, with no bed clothing of any description, I stretched myself for a nap. By about three o'clock, I found it necessary to turn out to the wood pile, and seek, in diligent chopping, the means of restoring the circulation, and, thereupon, I find the following entry:

Elmira, July 13th. Chopping wood, disgusting. If I had been that "Woodman," it would have required deuced little singing to have induced me to "spare that tree," or any other tree.

Day broke at last, and by at last, I essay to express the fact, that it seemed about as hard to break as Colonel N's passion for wearing clothes that wont fit him—and shortly after roll-call, I received a summons to the Major's tent. He offered me a cigar, which, having no small vices, I declined, and soon entered into a free conversation in matters military, political, and personal, concluding by handing me a note, which I found to be an assignment to duty in the office of his Adjutant. I reported at once, and was soon at work transferring to a large "Dooms-day Book," the record of the name, regiment, company, place and time of capture, ward and number of each prisoner, a volume which finally swelled to colossal proportions. I subsequently found that my position entitled me to a couple of cups of coffee, and a fee of—ten cents per diem ! The coffee was an anomalous production, made by suspending a bag of ground coffee (?) in a boiler holding, I presume, a hundred gallons, the water in which was renewed for three days, when the bag was taken out, emptied and re-filled. The first day's boiling was fair, the second unfair, the third a mockery and a delusion, but such as it was, I accepted it very thankfully, and considered myself entitled to make no complaint, as the Yankee Sergeants, in the pen, were furnished with the same.

In the course of a few days, the finances of the prisoners required attention, as money began to be sent them, and the Ledger was entrusted to my keeping, and ere long this business became so onerous that a reorganization of the Department took place; three professional book-keepers were employed, and a miscellaneous *role* of duty was assigned me—making out the morning death report, answering letters sent to the Major, making various enquiries respecting the camp, keeping the Sutler's daily accounts straight, and thrice a month, making out the "detail accounts" of the prison. As to this latter matter, Elmira forms an exception, I believe, to other Yankee prisons. All duty performed by prisoners, except the police of the quarters, that is, the daily cleansing of the camp, is paid for at the rate of five cents a day for mere laborers, and ten cents for clerks and artificers. These, workmen are divided into four heads, according as they report to the Adjutant, the Commissary, the Surgeon, or the officer commanding the labor detail, and as many as four hundred men in all are thus provided with employment, which relieves them of the horrible *ennui* of imprisonment, and furnishes them with the means of securing a moderate supply of tobacco—the universal consolation of *Lee's Miserables*.

I may add that the wages thus earned, were, in all cases, as far as I had the opportunity of knowing, honestly paid. I have a thousand times entered the credits on the Ledger to various prisoners, and have seen them draw out their deposites in the form of orders.

In the course of the various changes in my line of duty, I gradually acquired possession of a comfortable room, in which I soon rigged up a bunk, and, greatest blessing of all, formed, through the partiality of Capt. Whiton, an alimentary association with the Sergeant of the Cook-house, the chief Baker, and a pair of "rebs" engaged in those establishments, which secured me then, and thenceforth, against any apprehensions on the subject of rations, or any interest in the rise of rats.

This association with the officers commánding the prison, gave me, of course, many opportunities of assisting my fellow Confederates, and I had the happiness of being the means of making the stay of many of them less irksome, and their restraints less grievous to bear, without any compromise of their or my principles or position, which was known to be that of a rebel, *sans reproche.*

CHAPTER XVI.

Fearful Accident—Humanity of the Surgeons—The Main Chance —Preaching in Prison—Lynch Law—J. E. B. Stuart—Death in Prison—Scurvy—New Restrictions—Library—Digging Out.

I resume my extracts from my Diary, anticipating, occasionally, events of subsequent date, referring to the same subjects :

Saturday, July 16th. An ugly rumor prevails in camp, that a fearful accident occurred yesterday on the Erie Railroad—the train bringing prisoners here colliding with a coal train going east, near a place called, I think, Shohola. The deaths, it is said, number over fifty, and among them are several of the Yankee guards. To-night we were roused about mid-night, with a request that we would come and help the wounded in, the train having arrived with the surviving victims of the catastrophe. Many of them were in a horrible condition, and when I went to the Hospital, the following Monday, I found the wounds of many still undressed, even the blood not washed from their limbs, to which, in many instances, the clothing adhered, glued by the clotted gore ; still, the "Advertiser," the Administration paper in Elmira, of this morning, proclaims to the world that the poor fellows were humanely cared for! Lieutenant H., who visited them Tuesday, and who expressed to me his indignation in no measured terms, at the neglect, could tell a different story. An attempt was made to Court-Martial this officer, for acts of kindness to the prisoners, but he put a stop to all proceedings at once by intimating to the authorities, that in the event of a trial, he had a story to tell the *Herald* of the inhumanity of the Hospital treatment, at Elmira, which a trial would certainly force into print. *He was not molested.*

For many weeks afterwards, friends and relatives tried to obtain admission into the prison to see and administer aid to the sufferers, but were denied the privilege. In one case, a very near female relative made a trip of hundreds of miles to see a prisoner, and the only indulgence she received was a permission to ascend an observatory near "the pen" on a certain hour in the afternoon, when her kinsman was allowed to post himself under a tree in the enclosure with a white handkerchief around his arm, and thus, at a distance too great for any communication, they were allowed *to gaze at each other* for an hour! While I was at Elmira, I remember but two or three instances in which any one was allowed to visit a prisoner. A lady, by dint of great exertions, obtained from the authorities at Washington, permission to visit her son, who was badly wounded, and a clergyman, by officiating in "the pen," got the opportunity of a brief conversation with his son—one or two similar cases finished the chapter.

Wednesday, July 20th. Our curiosity has been excited for some days past, by noticing a wooden structure, consisting of two large platforms, one above the other, which has been going up across the road that bounds one face of our prison. I learn, to-day, that it is an "Observatory" where the sight-seeing penchant of the "Yanks" is to be made available, to put money in the purse "of an enterprising partnership, which proposes to turn our pen into a menagerie, and exhibit the inmates to the refined and valorous people of the Chemung valley, at the moderate fee of fifteen cents a head! "*Refreshments provided below.*"

The event justified the wisdom of the venture, for one of the proprietors, who was part of the management in our pen, assured me that the concern paid for itself in two weeks. I am surprised that Barnum has not taken the prisoners off the hands of Abe, divided them into companies, and carried them in caravans through the country, after the manner of Sesostris, and other antique heroes, turning an honest penny by the show.

So profitable was this peculiarly Yankee "institooshun," that a week or two thereafter a rival establishment, taller by a score of feet sprang up, and a grand "sight-seeing-and-spruce-beer" warfare began, which shook Elmira to its uttermost depths. One building was Radical, the other Copperhead; one was taller, the other older and more original—qualifications considered important by Dr. Sands, and quite as apropos to sight-seeing as to Sarsaparilla. Heaven knows where it all would have ended, but that the Government confiscated the "Democratic Platform," under the plea of military necessity, and its Abolition brother remained master of the situation.

Here every summer afternoon, the population of Elmira—chiefly of the female persuasion—congregated to feast their eyes on their enemies, much after the fashion that the worshippers of Dagon, mocked the mighty son of Manoah. and until the days became so cold, that exposure in so high a position was unpleasant, the shin plasters rolled in, and the lemon pop and ginger cakes rolled out of the orthodox observatory, to the great pecuniary comfort of the true-believers who owned it.

Sunday, July 24th. Major Colt suggested yesterday, that it might be desired by some of the prisoners to have divine service regularly on Sunday, and added that if an application were made out, he would forward it to Colonel Eastman, who commanded the post, and who would doubtless approve it. This was done, and the clergymen of the city readily assented to the proposition to visit the prison alternately. Under this arrangement we had service this evening, and almost every Sunday afternoon thereafter. The abolition editor in Elmira, complained very bitterly of the alacrity with which the clerical gentlemen accepted the proposal, and intimated that it was due to their *curiosity*, not their zeal—a little quarrel, I do not pretend to adjust.

Most of the clergy, who thus obeyed the scriptural injunction to "visit prisoners," conducted themselves properly, but we had a sample or two of the large lunatic wing of Northern orthodox—worthies of the Barebones type, who would above all things delight

"To prove their doctrines orthodox,
By apostolic blows and knocks."

Conspicuous among these was a fanatic named Brainerd, whose conduct was so disgusting that Lieutenant Richmond, heretofore, in this chronicle *honorably* mentioned, presented the worthy with *ten dollars*, in testimony of his appreciation! The joke was that Brainerd was fool enough to publish Richmond's letter in the Elmira B. R. organ—a gratuitous advertisement of a fool and a knave. *Arcades ambo.*

During the delivery of B.'s harangue some of his auditory quietly rose and left the presence of his abolitionship, whereupon Richmond arrested the non-comformists, and but for the intervention of another officer, would have clapped them in the guard-house, for the unpardonable sin of unwillingness to receive gratuitous insult. The clerical world in Puritan-dom, has not changed altogether from the happy days of Quaker whipping and Papist hanging, whereof the annals of Connecticut orthodoxy are rife. But while we may consider ourselves entitled to limited complaint on this score, it is proper to do justice to those who piously performed their functions, preaching, visiting the Hospitals, and furnishing those who desired them with religious books; and as falling particularly under my own observation, I may appropriately make my acknowledgements here to Bishop Timon, of Buffalo, Rev. Mr. Kavanaugh, of Elmira, and Rev. Mr. Hitselberger of Washington, whose attentions of this description were worthy all praise. Rev. A. Hull, D. D. of Elmira, was also untiring in his efforts to supply the moral and material wants of the prisoners. Aside from these regular services, no evening passed without prayer-meetings, conducted by the prisoners themselves, which were participated in with a decorum and devotion, which excited as much surprise as praise from our jailors, who during many months of service, at the same place, among the drafted men, had never known the torrent of Yankee profanity and obscenity, interrupted by the voice of prayer or praise.

Wednesday, July 27th. A sample of what used to be called in Scotia "Jeddart Justice,"—the ante-type of Lynch-law—amused us to-day. A miserable wretch was discovered picking the pocket of a dead man in one of the hospitals, when the "rebs" took him before Major Colt for punishment. The Major turned him over to his comrades, with *carte blanche*, to inflict any penalty short of killing or maiming him, so the Athenians met in the Agora, and soon resolved on his fate. A barrel-shirt was first procured, and the thief being invested with it, was trotted at a sharp double-quick up and down the camp, with hundreds of yelling followers, until he fell from exhaustion. He was then rested [?] by being ridden on a rail for an hour, with the same vociferous procession at his heels, and the offended majesty of justice was still further, and it is to be hoped, completely appeased, by launching him bodily at the end of this experiment into the filthy pool in the middle of the camp. He came out a much sadder, and infinitely dirtier, if not a better man.

There has been a rumor prevalent in camp for several days past, that certain informal peace negotiations have been going on in hearing of Niagara. To-day I obtained "by underground" a copy of the *Tribune* of a late date, in which the story is all told. When the facts come to be known about this war, the South will be surprised to find that there has been but one black republican, of any prominence in the North, who ever dared to open his lips for peace, and that was Greeley—conduct quite of a piece with the general vagaries of that tenant of the white coat and shocking hat, who has performed for a third of a century the dry-nursing of all the isms in Christendom—so, at least, say his enemies.

Wednesday, August 1st. Got an illustrated paper with a likeness and sketch of the life of General J. E. B. Stuart, this morning. A year ago to-day I was playing chess under a tree a mile or so to the left of Culpepper C. H., when a courier dashed up to General Mahone's tent, a few yards off, and in a moment, orderlies were hastening to regimental head-quarters, and the "long-roll" soon brought the brigade under arms. We had heard cannonading frequently during the day, and learned that the Yankee cavalry had crossed the Rappahannock, and were engaging our troopers who had been left to cover the rear of General Lee's army, then on its way to Orange. Anderson's Division brought up the rear of the infantry, and Mahone's Brigade the rear of the Division, so that we expected to move in the morning. It turned out, however, that the Yankees were too numerous for our cavalry to handle, and we were ordered to go to their relief. My own Regiment happened to head this movement, and we were double quicked at a pace not altogether comfortable, at 97 Fahrenheit, in the direction of the cannonading, which was now growing quite distinct and rapid. We soon came in sight of the belt of woods, which skirts on the West and South, that splendid plain on which the great cavalry review was held the year before, and the Yankees in force appearing, my Reigment with one from Posey's Brigade, was ordered to deploy as skirmishers, and advance through the woods. Then, for the last time, I saw Stuart. Gaily cantering along in command of the skirmishers, conspicuous from his fine person and horsemanship at all times—then, doubly so, since the only man on the field who was mounted—his coolness and good fortune attracted the attention of all. He was everywhere along the line, foremost of the foremost, cheering all by his encouraging words and his fearless conduct—humming an air, or giving an order with equal nonchalance, he looked

"From clanking spur to nodding plume,
A very star of chivalry."

There may be different opinions as to his capacity to manage large movements of cavalry— strange to say, there are not ten cavalry heroes in History—but of his individual courage, his presence of mind in danger, his burning devotion to the cause, his energy and his enterprising dash there can be no question. Praise from an officer of high rank in a different branch of service is always a sweet morsel to the soldier, and as we drove the Yankees to the river bank that evening, I saw many a jaded infantry-man, step out with a lighter pace and a firmer tread, as with hat in hand, the gallant trooper saluted our Regiment with "handsomely done boys—*are you not from Petersburg?*"

August 10th. A heavy mail from Dixie, which we can't get because some villainous "reb," made away with the Bulletin board last night! The Adjutant vows that until the plank comes back, the letters must lie in his desk, and great is our grief thereat.

August 11th. This morning the missing plank came back, ornamented with a well executed chequer-board, whereby some enterprising Confed. disgusted with prison monotony, doubtless supposed, he would be allowed in peace to regale himself. Three letters for me from home—a caballistic announcement in one of them, which was all Greek to the "Examiner," assures me that Petersburg is safe, and General Grant has been heavily punished "especially this morning," (July 30th.) This I afterwards learned to be the date of the explosion of the great Mine, when Mahone dealt such swift destruction on the doomed blacks.

One painful episode mars the record of this month. On the 21st of August, one of our comrades, a young man of irreproachable character, of intelligence and of a gentleness of manner, which won all hearts, even among the enemy, sank under an attack of intermittent fever, and died. Major Colt, who had been as considerate as possible during his illness, and who had permitted us to procure anything the town afforded that he needed, ordered a metallic coffin for him and allowed a hearse to enter the gates for the conveyance of the body to the Potter's Field, where the prisoners are accorded their stinted share of "God's Acre." Rev. Mr. Edey, a Confederate Chaplain, of one of the Texas regiments, and a decided rebel, though a native of New York, read the impressive service of the Episcopal church over the remains, while a little group of bare-headed men stood together around "the Dead House," in whose front the body lay. This over, we formed in procession behind the hearse, and marched as far as the prison gate—all the indulgence we could procure—with heavier hearts, I ween, and far more of genuine respect than has often marked the obsequies of King or Kaiser.

How many of us might make our exit from our prison bars on this wise, and who should be the next thus followed, were questions that did not fail to suggest themselves to all, and questions which kept some faces solemn for days thereafter.

August 25th. The sutler has been prohibited for some days back from selling any food to the prisoners, and the result is that fourteen hundred cases of scurvy are reported this morning! Some of them are very aggravated, and the symptoms are positively fearful. Men are loosing their teeth and hair, many have their bodies covered with sores, and their sinews so contracted as to prevent all locomotion, and in almost every instance these external symptoms are accompanied by disease of the stomach.

Only one Yankee grieves much at this—the sutler. His profits are thereby cut down considerably, and as his transactions usually amount to from two hundred to two hundred and fifty dollars per day, half of which, I presume, is profit, he is affected in a vital part, and is correspondingly comfortless. These physical evils are further increased by an order just received from Washington *confiscating* all food sent the prisoners, unless the Surgeon would certify that they were sick and in need of those articles, and all clothing, except "a change of under-clothing, and one outside suit of grey stuff and common material." Of course, the *confiscated* articles were generally *stolen*—the words being synonymous.

And thus the weeks rolled by. With the outside world we had little in common—cities were surrendered, States overrun, Conventions held, battles won, the immortal roll of glory received the names of Polk, Chambliss, Morgan, Rodes, Gregg, and to the vast record of the unnamed heroes, were added thousands as worthy of memory as the noblest of these. A new throne was set up on this continent—another turn in that great kaleidoscope which never changes the nature of one bead or bit of glass, be the changes in combinations of position ever so radical and numerous. But to us the book of events was sealed. Occasionally, by a bribe, we would achieve the reading of a newspaper, and hear in such partial phrase as prejudice affords, the story of the great tragedy our comrades were playing; but the last details, the points of personal interest—who was wounded, who promoted, who *dead* among those with whom we had shared march and camp, bivouac and battle-field—above all, what individual havoc the battering of our little city had occasioned—whom these sweet harbingers of union and amity, the shells of Grant, had sought out and destroyed; these were unanswered questions, big with import to us all.

Yet, a fairer summer never blessed the eye, and as we lolled on the grass in the long, dreamy autumn evenings, indulging *les delices du far niente*, nature seemed to whisper in every passing cloud and sighing breeze, a protest against the fatal strife that was desolating the land.

Early in September an addition was made to our comforts in the shape of a contribution on the part of some benevolent persons in New York, of two hundred or three hundred volumes wherewith a prison Library was formed, and the rush for reading was boundless. Of course, these volumes were as diligently expurgated as though the official " let it be printed" adorned the title-page, still, in our circumstances, a play-bill or a price current would have been interesting, and the shelves were soon denuded of every thing, down to infantile toy-books and dilapidated geographies.

During this month, two attempts at escape by tunnelling were made—the first a failure, the second successful. By the latter, eleven enterprising beavers made their escape, and the detachment sent after them returned in the midst of a snow which fell on the 5th of October, without having met a trace of the fugitives. They commenced digging in the middle of their tent, which was near an angle of the pen, and conveying the earth in blankets to the lagoon in the night, they avoided detection until a hole about thirty feet long and three feet in diameter was completed, under the fence, and on the first moon-less and cloudy night that offered they escaped.

CHAPTER XVII.

Exchange Rumors—The Negro Question—Too Healthy by Half—Application as Nurse—Paroled—Off for Dixie—Good Bye to Major Colt.

October 1st. For several days past, the rumor has been current in camp that an exchange of the sick and wounded on both sides is on the carpet, and the knowing ones are rubbing up their old complaints, getting their asthmas, rheumatisms, lame legs, &c., in working order for the examination about to take place. What wonder that many a paling eye flashes up now with unusual fire, and many a poor, feeble pulse, that for weeks past has been fighting an unequal battle with fever, starvation, memory and despair, bounds now with a fresh impetus, as in the distance, not very remote, there looms up the enchanting vision of wife and child, mother, sister—HOME. Many, alas! who are indulging themselves with this fair prospect will turn their trembling, tottering feet towards another home ere the light of the earthly one can answer their longings. *Pulsat pede.*

To-day the rumor takes definite shape as the Surgeons make their rounds through the wards examining the sick, and excluding from the roll all but those whose convalescence is apparent, and those who will never get better *here;* and it leaks out that the order from Washington is that a list must be made of those only who will be *unfit for duty for sixty days.* Having beat up Ireland,

Germany, Switzerland and Africa for recruits, these invincible twenty millions of Yanks admit that they are still not a match for five millions of Southerners, and they cling with the tenacity of Death to every able-bodied "reb" they can clutch, lest he may again enter the Southern army, where they well know he will overmatch any Yank that could be exchanged for him. The negro question, which they plead as their excuse for declining a general exchange, is all bosh of the first water. The Northern people, and I speak from long acquaintance with them, care infinitely less for negroes than we. The instinctive aversion with which all white races regard the blacks—an aversion which begins with the traditions of infancy, when "the big black man" is the bug-a-boo wherewith rebellious babyhood is terrified into obedience—is in the South modified, if not conquered, by constant association and the interchange of mutually serviceable offices. In the North, and wherever the white and negro live together in the ordinary condition of society as rivals in labor, competitors for employment, claimants for equality of privilege or contestants for a share of public patronage of any kind, the interests and instincts of the whites coalesce to intensify instinctive repulsion into interested hate, and a degree of intolerance exists, of which we in the South have no conception. It is the free States which have made the most odiously discriminating laws against the free blacks, and it is only in a free State that such bloody outbreaks against the negroes as have characterized Chicago and New York could possibly occur. It is not, therefore, black love but white fear, which is interposing difficulties in the way of a general barter of prisoners, and so controlling is this latter motive that the prisoners at Andersonville might forever have sung their sorrows to deaf ears, but for the advent of that crucible of parties and policies—election day. The McClellan men have proclaimed a general exchange as a plank in their platform and Humanitarianism—sorry I can't use a shorter word, but the difference between that and Humanity is as great as between Homousion and Homoiousion, which kept Christendom in hot water for generations—Humanitarianism, I therefore say, must have its sop. So the ingenious Yankees make a compromise between

Justice and Expediency by exchanging only those who will not be fit for fighting until the present campaign is over! and thus take the wind out of the Democratic sails, without sending a man to that army which the veracious Grant affirms is deserting to him at the rate of a Regiment a day!

Individually, my case is pitiable indeed. Full rations of beef, a quiet conscience and a good digestion, have left me in an awkward exuberance of health which precludes all hope of discharge on the ground of unfitness for duty for sixty days. Indeed, I am afraid that protracted residence here may induce a physical condition which even the example of Louis le Gros, Sobieski and Dixon H. Lewis could not reconcile me to, and I am forced, therefore, to seek an occasion of deliverance on grounds not hygienic. It occurs to me that it is incredible that so many *miserables* will be sent on a voyage South without attendants as nurses, and I am resolved to try the effect of an appeal for permission to accompany the sick in that capacity.

October 3rd. The hospital examinations completed, the search for unavailables began to-day in the wards. At 10 o'clock, the camp was mustered by companies, and Major Colt accompanied by the Medical Staff and a Clerk to record the names, made a careful inspection on this wise. The prisoners, by company, being in line, Major Colt gave notice, that all who desired to be examined, must step three paces to the front. Each man thus presenting himself was examined, and those found unfit by reason of age, or sickness or wounds, were recorded, while the rest were sent back sorrowing. This operation and the making out of the rolls occupied several days and nothing else was talked of, or thought of in camp. At last, on the 8th, the lists were completed, some fifteen hundred were found "unfit for duty for 60 days,"—one sixth of the whole—and on the morning of the 9th, notice was given that the "paroles" would be taken that day. No news had, up to this time, reached me as to the result of my application for detail as a nurse, and my hopes of deliverance received sundry rude shocks during the week from the announcement, confidentially made by one or two of the Yankee officers, that

I should be "the last rebel that should leave that pen," a distinction I was supposed to have attained by unusual bitterness of hostility to Yanks and Yankeedom,—Major Colt even honoring me, as I understand from a friend, by his *imprimatur* as *the worst " secesh "* in camp.

October 9th. Io triumphe! Evoe! A knock at my door ten minutes after 9; my friend D. calls me out with the gravity of a Lord Chancellor, and, *sotto voce*, announces "Major Colt has just put your name down on the list." Unfortunately the sumptuary regulations of the pen preclude the orthodox American fashion of expressing unlimited gratification, so I content myself with *feeling* as much joy as is consistent with sanity, and straightway go about disposing of my various unportable chattels among less favored friends—the universal concomitant of emigration.

Little was now done or talked of by any one except the approaching Hegira of the lucky candidates for exchange. Many a brawny fellow with the thews of Alcides would gladly exchange his exuberant health and perfect strength, for the most helpless frame and the puniest limbs in the hospital, and numberless expedients to elude the vigilance, or corrupt the integrity of the examiners were practiced—with what success I am not here to tell.

Numerous parole lists having been made out, the fortunate ones signed their names, either in person or by proxy, to an obligation whereby they bound themselves, not to take up arms against the United States, nor to perform any guard or other military duty in the field, or at any post or elsewhere, during the War until duly exchanged.

On the morning of the 11th, all being in readiness the fourteen hundred for exchange were called out alphabetically, and in three squads at different hours of the day, marched through the city from the pen to the Erie Railroad Depot, where two trains of box cars stood waiting.

I took leave of my companions, with the regret with which intimate association, such as that of prison, is sure to tinge the parting of the most callous, and from none with more than the excellent officer and gentleman who commanded the prison. His eyes filled as he bade me good-by at parting, and I fear my own were not altogether dry, as for the last time I wrung the hand of the true man, and humane, courteous official, Major Colt. He handed me a memorandum as we parted, asking my kind offices for Lieutenant-Colonel John R. Strang of his Regiment, and I almost felt regret at hearing of Colonel S.'s release subsequently, as it prevented me from reciprocating on my return home, in some slight degree, attentions and courtesies, which I in common with all my Petersburg comrades, had constantly received at the hands of this excellent officer.

CHAPTER XVIII.

Off for Baltimore—Contraband Communication—Point Lookout Again—Yankee Petty Larceny—Jackson's Valley Campaign—Diagnosis—Afloat—A Gallant Officer—Hampton Roads—Prizes and Prize Money—Hilton Head—Mitchel-town—Savannah—Home.

Our passage through Elmira did not excite quite the attention, which marked our journey through the same streets three months before, the curiosity of the Chemung Athenians having become satiated with such sights. Many citizens who dared to approach us with expressions of sympathy accompanied us to the cars, and ministered as they were able to the comfort of the most needy, but there was none of the obtrusive following and staring, with which we were honored on our first appearance.

It was nearly night fall when we were "all aboard," the

engines screamed and off we started for Dixie. We would scarcely have felt as much exhilaration had we known that the trip would take *a full month!*

The events of the next forty hours, consist in the dismal items of a creeping ride over the "Northern Central" Pennsylvania Railroad, which leaves the Erie Road at Southport, and traverses the most barren and uninteresting region of the Keystone State, through Harrisburg to the Maryland line, and on to Baltimore. I remember nothing particularly of this trip, except that whenever the train stopped, the guards robbed the nearest orchards; that I slept the first night in a space of three feet by six inches; that I consumed fabulous quantities of crackers; that when I got into Maryland, we found various flags flying in honor of the vote for emancipation, given the day before; that for slowness of movement, I'll match that ride against even the traditions of the "old City Point" road—a comparison which exhausts the resources of reproach; and finally that, after jolting enough to have killed twenty fashionables, we arrived in Baltimore on the morning of the 13th, about 10 o'clock, with seven corpses in the dead car—the first toll of the reaper.

A few ladies and children were at the depot—those who dared to brave the fines and dungeons, the imprisonment and insult, and exile, with which humanity and the natural yearnings of kin-ship are crushed out in *loyal* Baltimore; but, I doubt not, there were thousands of hearts in that fair town that day, who would have thought it the highest honor to have been allowed to minister to the sick and dying in our long trains, and were only restrained from coming by their unwillingness to witness sufferings that they could not alleviate, while the mere effort would compromise them, without aiding us. The train had hardly stopped, when a gorgeously caparisoned horse and Major dashed into the little crowd of ladies who were pressing around the car nearest the street, with enquiries about their relatives, and the less noble animal forced them back with a brutal sneer and an intimation in decided terms, that a renewal of the experiment of speaking to us, would infallibly result in their being sent to the common guard-house!

I was particularly sorry for this, as I desired to send a message to a friend in the city, and I resolved to evade the order prohibiting intercourse. Tearing a leaf from my note-book, I jotted down a few lines and rolling the letter in as small a compass as possible, I watched my opportunity when the guards were not looking in my direction, to hold it up with a gesture that attracted one of the ladies. As soon as a fair opportunity offered, I shot the "paper pellet" toward her, and was much gratified to observe the diplomatic nonchalance with which she put her foot on the missive, quietly continuing her conversation with a female friend meanwhile. A moment or two afterwards she *accidentally* let fall her handkerchief and stooping to recover it, picked up my note with it, and conveyed both to her pocket—all this without a look towards me. It was several minutes before she honored me with a glance of intelligence, which satisfied me my communication was in safer hands than any mail system in Christendom could furnish.

During the day, for it required all day to get us from the depot to the dock, several ladies remained near us; by strategem, entreaty—any means, and every means—conveying to the wretched inmates of our train, coffee, bread, cakes, fruit, tobacco—anything in short that money could buy, or woman's kindness of heart suggest. Among these a few were conspicuous in their zeal to serve us, and I remember best a courageous woman, with a true Baltimore face, dark eyes, a Southern complexion, lithe, graceful form, and features radiant and mobile with intelligence and beauty, and the divine glory of charity, who spent the long day in these ministrations, unawed by frowns, undismayed by threats, and conquering her native womanly disgust at the vulgar hirelings, that outstripped even Yankee heartlessness in the cruelty and brutality, with which they repulsed all efforts at communication with us. Her name in two hemispheres is the synonym of all that is noble, true and good, and from Pope's day to our own, has formed the best antithesis to

"——————— knaves and fools and cowards."

The sun was setting as I jumped on an ambulance well filled with hospital equipage, and rattled off to the wharf, where three steamers were awaiting us. That night about 10½, we started for Point Lookout, whence we are to be reshipped.

It was nearly dawn when I awoke to find our craft hard aground off Point Lookout; but soon the tide rose and we steamed up to the dock,—a heavy sea running.

Now commenced the troublesome and dangerous operation of getting the helpless sick ashore. A gangway plank was stretched from the side of the ship to two flour barrels standing on the dock, and down this "shute" the poor helpless, maimed creatures were slid like coal into a vault. Those of us who were able, spent our time in alleviating the roughness of this original process of debarkation, and assisted in placing the sick and wounded in the ambulances which conveyed them to the hospital a quarter of a mile distant.

Between the arrival of the first ship and the second, I walked to the hospital and deposited in the steward's room of No. 8, my "pack," expecting to return and get it when my duties on the wharf were over. Unluckily I did not get it for two days, and of course, when I recovered it, everything valuable was stolen. This petty larceny was committed by a smooth-faced innocent, with a downy upper lip, who at that time acted as orderly for Dr. Thompson, the Chief Surgeon of the post. Three weeks afterwards, Dr. Thompson returned me one or two of the articles stolen, but allowed (I presume) his underling to keep the rest. This at least I know, that I furnished Dr. Thompson with a full description of the stolen goods, some of which I saw his orderly wearing the day I finally left the Point, but never received any except a trifling proportion of the whole. All this I regretted, mainly, because I lost thereby several beautiful specimens of prison work that I was bringing home to my friends—and the only comfort I received from my comrades, was a sneer at my gullibility in leaving anything valuable out of my sight when Yankee soldiers were about.

Towards' night-fall, the sick and wounded who required treatment having all been removed to the hospitals, the remainder of the prisoners were marched to the old "officers' pen," and turned in with the suggestion that we make ourselves as comfortable as possible!—a rather grim joke that. While in line and before dismissal, I asked an officer who came with us from Elmira, to request permission for me to go and get my clothing, &c., left at the hospital. He was repulsed in so rude a manner by Major Brady, the commandant of the post, that he expressed to me his apprehensions that my property would certainly be stolen—a comfortable prophecy, as disagreeable as Cassandra's—*and as true.*

Three months had elapsed since I left this pen on my way to Elmira, and I congratulated myself no 'ittle on my early return, and on the near prospect of falsifying the prediction of the great representative thief, coward and brute of Massachusetts—now happily reporting at Lowell. Day after day, and week after week passed by, however, with no prospect of a move. While here, many prisoners came in from the army of General Early, in the Valley, whose demoralization was conspicuous. How different the story of this unfortunate campaign against Sheridan, with its long catalogue of robbery and disaster, from the glories with which the immortal Jackson illumined every hill-side of that long vale of the Shenandoah! When will that marvelous story be written? Is there no one with the genius to comprehend, and the bookcraft to do justice to that wondrous episode in this wondrous war—unparalleled save in the dazzling marvels of "The Campaign in Italy." Who will tell, in language worthy of the theme, how, with a few thousand infantry, poorly supplied with everything but valor and leadership, this illustrious captain swept army after army out of the field, defying numbers, annihilating distance, despising labor, regardless of odds, fairly revelling in the *gaudia certaminis—preferring* to have, it would seem, three armies to fight at the same time, that the glorious boys might not rust with idleness. Bravo as "Lion Heart," modest as Sydney, in action as impetuous as Ney, in counsel cautious as Fabius, reticent as Wellington, magnetic as Napoleon—there is not a meadow or mountain top in all that lovely valley that is not alive with tribute to this matchless chieftain, and yet, "History" hardly accords his grand campaign a paltry page, and his name which woke the echoes of two hemispheres seems doomed to find no more enduring monument than the ephemeral record of hasty pamphleteering, or the fading traditions of the camp fires!

Revenons! The days dragged very wearily here. As we were all nominally sick men, the facetious Yankees put us on sick diet or half rations, and as there was no sutler and no chance, therefore, of eking out our allowance, we began to fear our enemies were in a fair way of unfitting us for active service for the balance of the war. It seems that we are to be kept here until five thousand are accumulated, and then deported. Having no other occupation, I undertook some duties in connection with the hospital—for we had a hospital within the pen—and thus managed to endure the tedium of my cage by pious exercises in the shape of administering hospital slops and allopathic boluses.

In the midst of the pen was a pile of logs which the prisoners used as an observatory to get the earliest information of the arrival of the "New York," the truce boat of Colonel Mulford, U. S. Commissioner of Exchange, whose coming, it was thought, would ensure a speedy exit: but the Yankees took it into their sapient heads that there was something "irregular" in this, and our logs were pulled down and all spying put under the ban.

Wednesday, October 28th. An order came to *diagnose* us to-day, and it became necessary that every one should have a disease forthwith—at least on paper. We were accordingly called up and asked our various complaints: being still in a vulgar condition of health, it became necessary for me to catch a disease suddenly; accordingly, I soon became painfully afflicted, and when called on by the doctor, I drawled out a disease with a name as long as a Nantucket "sea sarpint," and was passed *nem. con.* This looks as though we were about to move, and Dixie stock is rising.

Sunday, October 31st. Saturday we had a false alarm. We were ordered out, inspected, examined, and marched down to the dock where, in the offing the Arctic, Baltic and Northern Light are lying, and "then marched back again," to our measureless and unspeakable disgust. But to-day, we are off in earnest. About 11 a. m., we were summoned into line, our names called, our blankets and all contraband clothing stolen from us, except in a few instances where the articles were worthless, and then we were conducted to the wharf where a small steamer received us "in lots," and conveyed us to the Northern Light, which, with steam up, was lying about a half a mile out. The other transports were already laden with the most helpless of the prisoners—those who in the first instance had been taken to the hospitals.

We scrambled up the side of the fine steamer, formerly a mail and passenger ship in the California trade, now a government transport in the employment of Uncle Abe, at one thousand dollars a day besides her coal, and were marched in various directions to the two lower decks of the ship, where hammocks of canvas had been slung in sufficient numbers to accommodate nine hundred men. Some twenty or thirty were separated by the Surgeon and kept on deck, for what purpose we never knew, and our little tug steamed ashore for another load. It was near night-fall when she returned, and as many of the prisoners were victims of night-blindness, I asked and obtained permission to assist them aboard, the dangerous footing of the ladder inspiring them with uncomfortable apprehension of a plunge overboard—and altho' Friar Peyton, told Henry VIII that the road to Heaven was as short by water as by land, the same is not as true of the road to Dixie.

I had helped the last one aboard when a handsome, frank-looking sailor with as genial a face as ever bent over a binnacle, tapped me on the shoulder and informed me that he wanted to see me "forrerd." My military habit of obedience, I presume it must have been, that induced my instant compliance and under the guide of Samuel H. Rich, 1st officer of the ship, I soon found myself in his cabin, scrutinizing the pattern of his furniture through an excellent glass—whose make, I never knew. From this time I, in common with all my fellow-prisoners who had any intercourse with him, had occasion to bless the day that we fell into the hands of so clever a gentleman and capital an officer. A young man but an old seaman, he had circumnavigated the globe a half a dozen times, be the same more or less, knew every foot of sea from Fulton Ferry to Van Dieman's Land, and possessed that ease of manner, that cosmopolitan heart and large fund of information and anecdote which, with thorough professional knowledge, forms the highest type of sailor —almost the highest type of the social man.

The management of the ship devolved on Mr. Rich, during our stay aboard, the captain being sick, and I had thereby occasion to observe the universal respect and good will which he commanded from the whole crew. These, by the way, were an exceptional party. There was not a Yankee among them, as far as I discovered, and a more liberal set of enemies would be hard to find. As I have spoken of the captain, (Lefebre) I may mention that he was the officer who commanded the Vanderbilt, when she was down in Hampton Roads, threatening destruction to our Merrimac. When the Merrimac threw all Yankeedom into such confusion early in 1862, Lincoln sent for Commodore Vanderbilt, to advise with him as to what was to be done with the monster. The Commodore informed him that there was no use trying to fight her, and the only chance was to run her down; but, as the United States possessed no vessel of sufficient tonnage for that achievement, he presented Lincoln with the Vanderbilt, a magnificent steamer of six thousand tons, and hurried to New York to put her in order for the great work. She had her upper works at once taken off, a formidable battery of heavy timber and cotton bales put in, enforcing her bows with thirty solid feet of structure, and a heavy casing of cotton

15

bales put around her boilers. In this trim she was sent down to Hampton Roads, and there lay for sixty days; but, as the Merrimac challenged the whole Yankee fleet for two days after her arrival, in vain, I presume the naval commandant at Fortress Monroe did not have as much faith as Vanderbilt, in the success of the running down project.

Monday, October 31st. Arrived off Old Point this morning. The harbor is filled with vessels of war, among which, I recognize the Minnesota, Susquehanna, Wabash, Shenandoah, Ironsides, and any number of iron-clads, "double-enders," &c., the whole floating, I understand, two thousand guns!

Commodore Lee has been superseded, on account, it is said, of too much love for the rebels, and Porter reigns in his stead. On each side, the war seems to have eliminated natives of the other from its service, until it has become a war of race rather than of institutions. Porter's vessel, the Malvern, lies a mile West of us.

We remained in Hampton Roads until Tuesday the 8th. The Atlantic and Baltic lay near us, and every morning we saw coffins going over the side in numbers, which suggested uncomfortable reflections on the uncertain tenure of life on a prison-ship. On the Atlantic alone, there were forty deaths during our stay in the harbor—a stay obviously unnecessary, and therefore, shamefully cruel, since it compelled the confinement of hundreds of sick men in the filthy and unventilated holds of large ships without proper food, medicine, or attendance. Captain Grey, of the Atlantic, protests loudly against the inhumanity of the proceedure, but circumlocution must have time. On the 2nd and 3rd, we were visited by a furious storm, during which Commodore Porter steamed up to Portsmouth, out of the reach of danger, and there remained until Saturday. On the 4th, Butler left for New York, whither he goes to keep the peace! The crew of our ship are from New York, principally, and all McClellan men—their indignation at having the Brute sent to overawe their friends of "the bloody Sixth," is quite refreshing, and they freely promise him a merry time if he interferes. They are mistaken—no race ever bowed the knee to bayonets with such edifying humility as the Yankees.

Saturday, 5th. The New York, Colonel Mulford's "exchange" boat is alongside the wharf to-day, and any number of rumors fill the ship, of speedy departure. These are confirmed somewhat by the arrival of Mr. Beebee, Agent of the Sanitary Commission, with large supplies for the Yankee prisoners, who will be received in exchange for us. Some of these supplies failed to reach Savannah, as the guards broke into the treasure to-night, and all got gloriously drunk on the liquid contributions of the Commission.

Sunday 6th. A prize steamer loaded with cotton came in to-day, and two more during the week. These vessels with their cargoes are sold after condemnation by a prize court, and half the proceeds turned over to the government. One-twentieth of the remaining half goes to the commandant of the North Atlantic squadron, and the rest is divided among the officers and crew of the capturing vessel. Under this rule, it is estimated that Porter's share of prize-money, while on duty here up to this time—about twenty-five days—will amount to twenty thousand dollars. Last night we were aroused by an indiscriminate firing throughout the fleet, and on getting on deck, found the harbor ablaze with colored lights, and guns going off in every direction—a sham naval battle at night. This, and the constant drilling at the guns, with the daily practice of launch-drill, indicate an early and vigorous naval attack in some direction—probably Wilmington, and as an armada is accumulating here, already more powerful than any ever set afloat from the days of the Argonauts, we may look for a powerful blow, when it is delivered. Boat loads of soldiers are constantly passing down the river. These are patriots of the right political stripe, who are being furloughed to go home to vote—"no other need apply."

At 4½ on the evening of Tuesday the 8th, we weighed anchor, and in company with the Atlantic, Baltic, Illinois, Herman Livingstone, and two or three empty transports, we started for Hilton Head, where we arrived about 9 o'clock Thursday night. This, as the world knows, is the *point d'appui* of the military operations of the enemy in South Carolina.

Quite a village has sprung up in the harbor, and about a mile north of this is Mitchell-town, named after the astronomer General, who left his appropriate star-gazing in the Cincinnati Observatory to civilize Southern barbarians. But their country revenged their wrongs, by poisoning his blood, and that of "many a tyrant since," with the deadly malaria of the coast, and so ended that and all other mundane business for the "astronomer-royal" of Porkopolis.

Mitchell-town is quite an interesting locality, as the scene of a grand educational and civilizing experiment on the blacks whereby the problem of the improvability of that singular race was sought to be solved. And, singular, indeed they are. For at least forty centuries they have held undisputed possession of a continent, and yet their passing generations have not left a trace on the page of history. Time has overflowed with miracles of human achievement, wherever else man's foot has trod; but here, there is only a dreary blank. In all these teeming centuries, *they* have stood still. They have written no book, painted no picture, carved no statue, built no temple, established no laws, launched no ships, developed no language, achieved no invention. The wisdom of the Egyptians was at their door, and they lit no lamps from that bright torch. The Arab startled Europe with his advances in mathematics and natural science, filling the northern sky of Africa with an aurora of scientific light—but its ray could not penetrate the invincible ignorance of the Ethiopian. Christianity was planted there by martyrs of the apostolic age, and stifled and died in the mephitic air. Civilization, upheld by the concurrent efforts of the most powerful states, succumbed to influences more powerful than arms, treasures and fanaticism combined, and the African stands to day, as did his ancestors in the days of the Pharoahs, a moral and physical mystery in the earth—

the victim of some dread judgment of God, powerful, searching, pervasive, and, it would seem, irreversible. Let us return to the Mitchel town *fiasco*. Every one knows the result. Several packages of first class Yankee school marms were exported to Mitchell-town, armed with acres of spelling books, pinafores, slate-pencils and sugar candy, for the reclaiming of the unregenerate Pompeys and pickaninnies of South Carolina, and divers bulbous Sleeks and attenuated Pogrims, electrified the world with the wonders—to come. Monthly reports kept alive the excitement, and monthly contributions kept alive the reports, until a half a year having elapsed, it leaked out that the "marms," had with singular unanimity resolved upon a grand and unusual act of consecration to the cause, to which the Hindoo "suttee" is not a circumstance. Pursuing their martyr-like resolve to devote themselves entirely to the elevation of the poor b'acks, they magnanimously determined to waive all paltry prejudices as to color, and a general amalgamation ensued and—and—in short, school teaching became soon entirely out of the question. Poor school marms! They were incontinently dismissed by the heartless government, and the elevation of the unbleached received a mortal blow. Pitiable indeed was the case of these Connecticut martyrs, and miserably cruel the conduct of Uncle Sam. Verily, verily, republics *are* ungrateful. Nothing is left to these missionaries of civilization except the reward of a satisfied conscience, and that consolation which springs from the faithful discharge of maternal duties.

We lay in this roadstead until Saturday, when orders came to proceed as near as possible to Fort Pulaski, and in a few hours, we were safely moored along side the single Yankee gunboat, which kept watch and ward over the entrance to the Savannah river, and which, by the way, was covered to the tops with a strong netting to prevent enterprising rebels from boarding and capturing her, by one of those "horse marine" movements, which have been among the most amusing and most successful feats of the War.

We lay here all night—a soft, summery night, though late in the fall, and many of us lounged on deck till morning, too much exhilarated by the safe termination of our captivity and the near approach of home, to waste our hours in the prosaic stupidity of sleep. Major Abrahams, the officer in charge of us, and Lieut. Gordon, both of the 85th Penn., I met frequently while pacing the deck, and found them quite as anxious to deliver us, as we to be delivered. Their terms of service had expired, and they were pressed into this service by a piece of military smartness—which is not wisdom either side of the line—in order that some duty might be extorted from them after the legal claim of the Government had expired. Early next morning, the Exchange boat, "New York," with Colonel John E. Mulford, Commissioner, aboard, came alongside; we were hurried aboard, and with three rousing cheers for the Northern Light and her officers and crew, steamed up stream to the truce ground, some ten miles up the river. Here we were met by a deputation of citizens and a squad of that excellent society of Good Samaritans, who have succored the soldier on every field and under all circumstances, from the Spring of 1862 to this day, the Richmond Ambulance Committee, and transferring ourselves with commendable speed—*for invalids*—to an aboriginal craft composed of a railroad shed mortised into a flat boat, we were soon puffing at a safe speed to Savannah.

It was near mid-day when we arrived here, amid the enthusiastic shouts of the people and the enlivening music of a genuine Southern band, vocal with "Dixie."

How joyfully and well those citizens met us, who sixty days thereafter passed such extremely "loyal" resolutions at the bidding of Tecumseh Sherman, it is not pleasant now to dwell upon. Sixty days are an æon in these times.

Our arrival was the signal for a general massacre of all bipeds furnished with feathers, in that vicinage, and the prisoners fared sumptuously once more.

Savannah is the most beautiful Atlantic city of the South, and we found in her long level streets and her spacious and elegant squares agreeable means of passing our walking hours. An interview with General McLaws enabled me to obtain passes for my fellow "militia men" and myself, and the next evening I bade adieu to Georgia. After numberless and most perilous adventures, such as infallibly befall those who go down into the land in railroad cars, I arrived in Petersburg on the night of Thursday—tired, hungry and unkempt, but profoundly grateful withal to that over-ruling Providence had preserved me unharmed amid the perils of Yankee pickets, the raging ocean, and the Piedmont Railroad.

An imperial autumn moon was flooding the earth with a sea of silver sheen, chequering the city with its sleepy contrasts of dreamy lights and bold, deep shadows, as I trod its deserted streets, ploughed in many a quarter with the track of the crushing shell and shot; and the sharp perpetual ring of the picket's rifle, gave its martial echo to every foot-fall that pressed the pavement. Everything suggested strife, contest, and the wreck and desolation of war. I passed the churches and found that their yards had been converted into burial grounds—the public cemetery being within reach of the enemy's guns, and therefore unapproachable. In many private grounds I noticed embankments with which bomb-proofs were covered, for the safety of the citizens during the frequent bombardments. Many of the lower stories of dwellings were protected by barricades of cotton bales: on every side, in a word, were monuments at once of the perils and the fortitude of the gallant people, who, through a siege of nine months, during which they have suffered every extremity of war, save famine, and almost that, have nobly and without the first murmur of complaint, devoted themselves and their all to the cause, *coveting*, as it were, the honor of civic martyrdom, from which so many others have meanly shrunk. Well and worthily did the noble little town win her title of "Cockade" in 1812; and nobler and more indisputable is her right to the distinction now.

How suggestive was all this! In leaving prison, I found I had not come to peace, but to the presence and the centre of war, and I read in the melancholy but mute lessons of the solemn, silent tombs that started like unbidden ghosts out of the shadow of each house of worship, the record of mortal dangers, not to men alone, but to inoffensive and helpless women and children. Still there required no subtle philosophy to find abundant consolation amid all this—was I not with each step of my hurrying feet, fast approaching, nearer and nearer, to the welcome and the warmth of the lips and hearts and hearth of Home?

www.ingramcontent.com/pod-product-compliance
Lightning Source LLC
Chambersburg PA
CBHW020112170426
43199CB00009B/505